HOW TO...

# WRITE A BOOK

# IN 53 DAYS!!

The

## ELEMENTS of *SPEED WRITING*
## NECESSITY & BENEFITS too!

by
Don Paul

Book Cover Design
by
Sunny Woods Paul

**How to produce, publish and sell
a great book during a vacation.**

## BOOK I

ISBN 0938263-10-2

# Path Finder Publications

1296 E Gibson Rd, E-301   Woodland, Calif 95695

© **Don Paul and Path Finder.** *Wir werden es bald auch auf Deutsch drücken.  Reservamos las derechas de publicar en Espanol.*

**Copyright**, Don Paul and Path Finder Publications, 1992

## Publisher's Cataloging in Publication
### *(Prepared by Quality Book, Inc.)*

Paul, Don 1937-
    How to write a book in 53 days : the elements of speed writing, necessity and benefits, too! / by Don Paul ; book cover design by Sunny Woods Paul.
        p. cm.
    "How to produce, publish and sell a great book during a vacation" -- t.p.
    Includes index.
    ISBN# 0938263-10-2
        1. Authorship. 2. Composition (Language Arts)--Guide books  3. English language--written English. I. Title. II. Title: How to write a book in fifty-three days. III. Title: Elements of speed writing.

PN147.P3 1992                    808.042
                                 QB192-33

**Library of Congress Catalog Card Number** 92-80122
**ISBN#** 0938263-10-2

# HOW TO WRITE A BOOK IN 53 DAYS!!
## Table of Contents

### Section I
**Part time, or 23 days of solid preparation.**

### Section II
**Setting your clock and getting ready to start**

# BOOK II

**Hitting the keys—hard and fast.**
**The buck starts here. Adding extra attractions.**

**1.** TAKING CAREFUL AIM AT YOUR TARGET AUDIENCE. Polling your
readership. Who'll read you, male or female? Young or old?
**2.** KICKING THE KEYBOARD TO PRODUCE MARVELOUS
MANUSCRIPT. Super-speedy manuscript tricks. How to create special
attraction with word-emphasis.
**3.** AUTOMATIC PRODUCTION Tossing tedious and vital book parts
together with the push of a button.
**4.** ADD THOUSANDS OF EZ WORDS. PICTURE POWER. Add pizazz.
How to draw and photo for super selling punch. How captions make a
super selling book. High production with super-paint. Graphics Integration.
**5** CREATE A THINK-TANK TO CREATE—-A PERFECT MANUSCRIPT.
Fine comb your manuscript at almost no cost. With better expertise than a
New York publisher, let outside experts re-work and polish your book.
**6.** HOW TO DO WORD-WORK & PRODUCE FINE LITERATURE.
Minor modifications, deletions and additions put power in your manuscript.
How to position your best for maximum impact.
**7.** THE WONDER OF CAMERA READY MANUSCRIPT. Book-birthing
made easy. How to create ultimate baby book beauty.
**8.** MAKE BROWSERS FIND LOVE AT 1st SIGHT. TITLES AND
COVERS. Create a lure on your book cover. How to find back cover
zingers to clinch sales. How to understand color influence.
**9.** TOOLS OF THE TRADE. High caliber guns to shoot words like bullets.
Tricks on setting up cheap to produce top quality.

Introducing. . .

## PATH FINDER PUBLICATIONS

Path Finder began when we first invented a way never to get lost in the woods without using a map; it's called, _The Green Beret's Compass Course, Never Get lost._ Over 31,000 copies are in print.

Next, we added to our book list and widened our distribution. We published:

> _The Green Beret's Guide to Outdoor Survival_
> _Everybody's Knife Bible_
> _Great Livin' in Grubby Times_
> _24+ Ways to Use Your Hammock in the Field_

We developed and wrote about all kinds of new ideas and outdoor methods. We're the people who figured out and published:

√A 30¢ two ounce wilderness bed for sleeping above ground.

√The modification for your hunting knife sheath which enables you to see the floor of a jungle at night.

√A new shooting system to give you super bullet placement, day or night.

√Life saving, simple procedures for self defense.

√Terrain analysis for saving energy as you travel on foot over rough country.

√A new cold-weather survival method to keep you alive anywhere.

√A guide to water purification for any survivalist.

√How to use animals to double your survive-ability.

√Green Beret team concepts applied to survival groups so you can enjoy the ultimate life-style outdoors.

√How to use a Hammock to trap food, net fish, & camouflage anything

i

All of our books have gone into multiple editions. Many people consider them the finest outdoor how-to books in the world. We've been represented by over 500 dealers and we've supplied our books by mail order to outdoorsmen from all over.

## (See the order coupons in the back of this book.)

Most major outdoor magazines have reviewed us. Our books are guaranteed for life. Should you destroy your copy or need an upgrade, you can obtain a brand new, updated copy for half price, plus what's left of your old copy.

On deck for Path Finder as of 1 Jan 92:

Book II of this "Elements-of-Speed" series. We've already manuscripted chapters included in this book's table of contents.

Also, **Speed Spanish for Gringos**. We'll get you fluent in 27 days with an all new system for easy learning. Did you know that all the "tion" words translate into Spanish as "cion" words? That may be no big surprise, but you might be pleased to know that all the "cion" words in Spanish convert easily to verbs (mostly "ar" verbs. I can teach you to use any verb in past, present and future tenses in under 10 minutes. This book promises to be **good fun, easy learning**, and above all, **fast fluency**. Publication date: NLT June 92. Look for me as you drive into Tijuana. I'll be the gringo on the donkey just south of the border who's hawking the book unless my wife and I get a better deal on a cruise ship.

Mail to:

## Path Finder Publications

1296 E. Gibson Rd., Suite 301  Woodland, Calif.  95695

Hang on now, and let us show you how to write a book just about like this one---in only 53 Days!

# HOW TO WRITE A BOOK IN 53 DAYS

## INTRODUCTION

## WHY THIS BOOK
## WILL MAKE YOU A GREAT WRITER

In 1980, I began writing seriously after I paid about $10,000 for a CPM computer and printer. I had previously written and published magazine articles, but I didn't like the profession because re-typing the same article over and over was not my idea of a good time.

But computers radically changed things. They turned the job of monotonous re-typing into the thrill of creating a masterpiece. Just as in the finest woodworking, writers could now direct their energy into polishing until their word-work dazzled both the eye and the mind.

To date, my published books provide me with good income from their sales successes. When you look through this book, you'll learn tricks of the writing trade that will boost your sales and income. But that's OK. There's lots of room for pro in the writing field. This book was fun to write. It ought to be fun to read, too.

When I tell you how to choose a hot-selling subject, you'll see how: I searched the market for a need, then worked up a salable outline, then checked the competition, then arrived at a "go" for the manuscript. The text of this book shows you how to extract your best to make sales-alluring back-cover material. Hopefully, our back cover does that well. Moreover, we show you how to present that best with page layout and word emphasis. You'll be able to see the cover lettering and follow the point and font sets just as if you did them for word emphasis yourself. I'll show you how to clamshell your outline and move each part of it so it gives birth to a chapter in your book. You'll see how each chapter sticks together and recognize the results. I'll show you how to collect, modify and import humor in order to put sparkle in your writing. This book contains a lot of funny samples. You can laugh 'n learn.

But before we start, please stand and bow your head in prayer as we acknowledge one of our greatest writers, poor James A. Michener.

He confessed he wrote all his books slowly, with two fingers on an old typewriter, rewriting up to six or seven times. HAWAII went very slowly and needed constant revision. Since the final draft contained a half million words, he typed over three million! He holed up in a phone-less Waikiki room and wrote seven days a week for a year and a half.

After I wrote this, here's what happened with Michener: I called his office in Coral Gables and asked for an OK on the quote above. "No problem." Then, I decided to send a manuscript. When I thought it over though, I got a better idea. I wrote and offered to come to Florida, set up a computer and teach him to speed on a literary freeway. I got back a letter from some secretary telling me he was over eighty and not interested in speed writing.

Granted, work is the price we pay for money, and the final draft was great. But, how my heart aches for any man who suffers like that. Michener lived only two minutes from a surfing paradise he didn't take time to enjoy. What a sacrifice! What a struggle!

"Dear God in Heaven, may we never have to pay a price that high. Amen."

How about you?

```
Would you like to double your income,
On the best days off you ever took?
Then, take an eight week vacation,
And pump out a first class book.
```

You can knock out a book faster and more easily than you ever thought possible. Computers help, of course, and the new softwares truly make magic. But the keys to supersonic speed are the tips and tricks laid out in these pages.

Will your word-work sell? Almost anything you ever learned or experienced can be shared for profit. If your life has been full of experience and you have studied, you own a brain bank account full of knowledge. Just publish a book on what you know, whom you know, where you've been or what you can do.

For example, I can speak Spanish fluently. I learned in high-school over 35 years ago. While I was learning the language, I learned HOW TO learn a language. Thus, slated for Jan 92 release: SPEED SPANISH FOR GRINGOS. Think of the potential. We can teach you fluent Spanish faster than anyone. Might we sell libraries, cruise ships and every tourist spot south of the border?

Even if your book doesn't break sales records, you score. Most authors are held in high esteem. Write on any subject, and most people will regard you an authority in that field. If you happen to write about your own profession, you become an expert.

For example, Attorneys and real estate brokers who write something clever about their practice gain popular appeal. The income boost from your increased status often creates an increase in business to compliment the bucks you make on your book.

To date, I have written and published five books. I also wrote two as yet un-published Tactical Tennis books. When Rambo became popular, I traveled all over the Pacific to interview other Green Berets and gather the material for new and advanced outdoor systems. I wrote:

THE GREEN BERET'S COMPASS COURSE.
THE GREEN BERETS' OUTDOOR SURVIVAL, I&II
EVERYBODY'S KNIFE BIBLE
24+ WAY TO USE YOUR HAMMOCK IN THE FIELD
GREAT LIVIN' IN GRUBBY TIMES

With the Green Beret Books, I missed the wave like a disappointed surfer. It took me too long to write, draw, collate, and print. By the time my books began to sell, the "Rambo-rush" was over. Even though sales improved again during Desert Storm, that experience was my first clue to the importance of literary velocity.You can learn the same lesson a lot cheaper.

> TO MAKE MONEY IN THE WRITING GAME,
> YOU HAVE TO BE QUICK.

Can I teach you speed? You bet. I've been writing books and magazine articles for over ten years. The shortcuts in this book teach you how to create some of the tedious parts of the book automatically. You'll bypass a lot of work. The systems are tested, and our results are published right—right before your eyes.

I finished the first rough draft (sans illustrations) for this book in twelve days. YOU'LL BE ABLE TO DO THE SAME. I am about to teach you how to produce hot copy while rocketing along on a great literary trip. Let's do it!

TO BEST USE THIS BOOK:
This is a "read-as-you-need" deal. First, scan my outline and decide what you need to know.

BOOK I deals with preliminaries. That's stuff you do before you go away to write somewhere. You develop a list of possible subjects you might write about and check them out. Then you choose from your subject list to make sure you start out writing with a winner. You organize, then add a little extra material from research. Start thinking about your project; hold and record those thoughts. We show you how.

This book also tells you how to plan and prepare your writing schedule, sets you up to write with full concentration, and teaches you how to add the special pizzazz of humor and a hot table of contents.

BOOK II deals with the actual writing of your book, the heart of the matter. If you already know how to outline, research, insert humor and think the project through, start with BOOK II where the fingers smack the keyboard. After that, send for test read, edit, re-edit, add pictures, do your covers up in style, and bring it all together.

I can teach you speed. For blinding speed, however, you need a modern vehicle. Horse 'n buggy typewriters will slow you down. Think about learning to word process on a computer. If you aren't familiar with computers and the writers' world of software, take a look at the last chapters first. Many writers who use typewriters think of a computer as the beast, but if you want to last in this game and compete with the new writers coming up, switch. Then keep up with new technology as it comes along.

In most of my books, I explain a lot of how-to from my own experience, but I use the word, "we." It's not only an anti-vanity euphemism, but it gives credit to my helpers---computer, CD Rom player, and Modem.

Note: As we venture into the mechanics of speed, we'll show you some computer commands. The brackets or parenthesis we use to surround those commands will tell you which computer we refer to. Copy these out of the book and post them on a wall for easy reference as you read.

**WORD PERFECT COMMANDS:** < >.
**WORDSTAR COMMANDS:**        [ ].
   **MAC COMMANDS:**              { }.

Note this also:  The brackets  only set the commands apart from my text.  For any command using an IBM clone we use the ^ to designate the control key.  For the MACINTOSH, we write Apple to mean the key which most approximates "#" as well as the apple sign (on most keyboards).

Also, take a look at the font notes:  I changed fonts and sizes for each chapter.  The test of a good font and size is how easy it reads.  Time your reading speed by the page.  It will help you to learn whether sans-seriff or seriff fonts are easier on your eyes. Probably, what's good for you will be just fine for your reader.

Now let's blast off!

*The above printed in boring, but easy to read  Helvetica, 10 pt fonts.  Poetry in 14 pt Jott.  Leading standard.*

6

## Chapter 1

## WHY SPEED IS MORE IMPORTANT
## THAN ANY OTHER WRITING SKILL

If you want to sell words, be a rapid-writer. Learn speed! The benefits are enormous.

You'll get to market on time.
You'll beat any competition to the market.
You'll prevent writer's block.
You'll produce more (therefore, earn more).
You'll learn to write better (more practice).
Why should you write two books a year when it's just about as easy to write four? Lots of

**BOOK PRODUCTION.** The quicker you write, the more you produce. The more you produce, the quicker and better you get at writing. When you become quick and good, you earn tremendous bucks.

writers have back-burner subjects they can't get to because they are held up in production with a current project.

## SPEED IS CRUCIAL TO SUCCESS!

Around 1981, I completed my first book. I invented a way to get around in the woods without getting lost. It worked great; you could bee-line right back to where you started from without using a map. We just completed our sixth edition, to which we added extra material. So now---we have 50,000 words, and the price has gone from $4 to $10.

Looking back, our publication format was poor. But we sold earlier copies at a low price and we still kept people from getting lost. That may have saved a number of lives. Here's the bottom line: Write and publish what you know now. Charge fairly. After you sell out, research, rewrite and expand with information and drawings to make a bigger, better book.

In 1981, The American Handgunner Magazine published my first major magazine article. I was happy, but I don't know why. Over three weeks, I polished those 2,000 words nine times. Since I wrote it on a typewriter, re-writing meant retyping. After spending $34 on photos, I wrote 20,000 words for $166. That's under a penny a word, or $55 a week. I learned from that. If the point of writing is to produce saleable copy you can sell at a profit, you have to be quick.

> **Be quick!  Otherwise you'll find yourself reading someone else's book on your subject.**

Today in modern America, the pace is rapid. Few topics are timeless. Yesterday's literary hits are today's garage sale left-overs. If you have something to write, you can't afford delay. You'll never earn a living if it takes too long to put your stuff together, because no book sells well unless it hits the market while the subject is hot and in demand. A timely hit with errors will earn a lot more money than a perfect book about old know-how.

Later, I'll teach you how to choose a saleable topic to write about. Will your book be a hit or a miss? All factors considered, the major determinant for success or failure is timing. You have to get your book out and on the retailers' shelves while the subject matter is still hot. Manuscript perfection doesn't mean much; **quick production means a lot.**

Consider this book. I had an exclusive subject to write about. Like many writers, I've studied *The Elements of Style*. After I bought my first computer, I started to play a game against myself called, "How fast can you write?" That was the lab course for learning these tricks, *The Elements of Speed.*

Have you noticed how fast new knowledge comes in and out of vogue? Remember when we all played Scrabble, Backgammon? To make money on those subjects, you had to be quick.

Not only does your book have to land on the market when people want to know. You also have to worry about competition. You're not the only writer out there who is constantly looking at modern trends because she is selling information.

## PREVENT WRITER'S BLOCK

Speed writing also overcomes fear of failure. Given a sufficient lapse of time between a book's beginning and ending, human frailty takes over and you think up excuses for not writing, such as, "Nobody will like this, or, my writing isn't perfect enough."

Writer's block definition: A parasitic disease which enters writers' brains and destroys their nerve. Acquired from old manuscripts. Cure is often impossible. Prevention is the only prudent course of action.

Writing anything appears as a formidable job. But speed writing makes the task much easier. If you don't learn to write fast, every book or script you ever attempt will appear on the horizon of your mind like an iceberg. Awesome! You think it will take years to produce. Slow writers regard the task that way, and it often causes writer's block.

Many people regard writers as ladies and gentlemen of leisure who live off royalties. A better definition might be: Published writers are determined, hard workers who survive rejection and keep on pumping out manuscript in the face of big time rejection. Would-be writers haven't learned determination yet, and the fear of rejection stops them dead on their keyboard. Books they dream about appear as mountains they're afraid to climb.

## MINIMIZE THE TASK

Quite a few people who know how to write...don't. That's because they took better paying, steadier jobs. "I would write," they tell me, "but I don't have time." That's too bad. We fly through time on a freeway. We slide in and out of fast food eateries. But somehow, we think it takes forever to write and publish something. Hopefully, this book might change that.

> To produce 120 pages, you could write for 8 days and complete 15 pages a day. Fifteen pages contain about 6,000 words, which is two hours at 50 words per minute---an easy speed to type if you write over a well developed outline.

Just as with mountains, the task of writing APPEARS to be immense. APPEARS. But as we all know, the angle of any mountain slope changes with perspective. Once you are climbing, it doesn't seem so tough. Writing is the same. But how do you finish the climb? Just start--and don't stop--until you're on top.

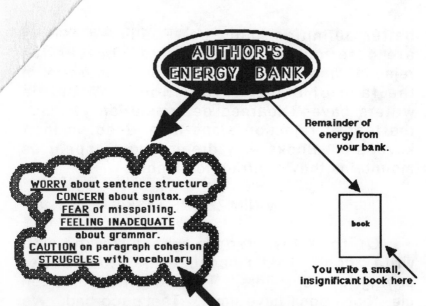

AUTHOR'S ENERGY BANK

Remainder of energy from your bank.

WORRY about sentence structure
CONCERN about syntax.
FEAR of misspelling.
FEELING INADEQUATE
about grammar.
CAUTION on paragraph cohesion
STRUGGLES with vocabulary

book

You write a small, insignificant book here.

If your energy drain off is this big here...

Never let your manuscripts age. Simply go for it. Follow the flow until you produce the whole book. Sure, this book is full of mechanical wonder works to jet you over a lot of writing difficulties. But, when it comes the final reality, you alone face the keyboard---all by your lonely self. Either you win or the computer makes you run and hide. You can go to the beach, fish, hunt, play tennis and goof off all you want, but, honey, when you come home, the computer is still there. Face it. Hit the keys.

> You can't write profitably if you don't write fast. Any extra time you spend writing and collating keeps your book off the market.

We are "authors." Keyboards don't make cowards out of us. Few people believe this, but authors is an acronym standing for: **A**nonymous **U**nderlings **T**o **H**arness **O**ur **R**esources **S**peedily. You wanna write? Get with it. Make a conscious choice to win or you automatically choose to lose. Don't hesitate. Start now! If you have something saleable to say, put it together quick and sell it.

### WHAT KEEPS US FROM WRITING FAST?

What stops some writers from producing copy is this: The false notion that saleable word-work must conform to someone else's idea of perfection. Do you think your writing isn't good if it has mistakes in it?

Books about punctuation, grammar mechanics, and syntax often cause us to carry some terrible English baggage around. "Never end a sentence with a preposition. Don't use 'ain't.'" Forget that! A good number of books and schools miss the point. Sure, English composition basics are important. But, those basics are nowhere near as important as writing quickly. As a matter of fact, dwelling on those basics has created negative ability in a lot of students. The kid had something to say, but she was convinced she didn't know how.

Attention to petty details not only slows you down, but makes the writing task <u>seem</u> beyond your ability.

WHY MANY WRITERS WITH POTENTIAL NEVER PRODUCE

Too much confusion reigns about where this thing goes. Therefore, the writer worries and loses concentration on good writing.

But fear of making "a mistake" only slows you down, creates mental blocks, and pulls you away from concentrating on style and substance. Don't let anyone convince you that writing well is beyond your ability.

Set your mind free from the constraints of writing correctly. Go for production---and you can use your wit, articulation, sarcasm and humor like a branding iron. Stay on your natural writer's high, the ultimate creative motivator. Don't bog down in a quagmire of mechanical detail.

**Your concentration ability has limits. Learn to use 100% of that vital ability.** You write your best when **all** of your ability goes into your manuscript. Allowing yourself to get sidetracked with petty details such as grammar, sentence structure or spelling will detract from the punch and sparkle of your main message. Attention to detail only throws you off the path of creativity. Do you **really want to communicate?** Concentrate on the right stuff.

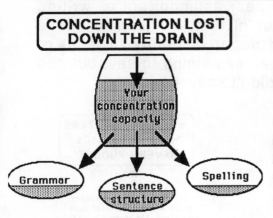

CONCENTRATION LOST
DOWN THE DRAIN

Your concentration capacity

Grammar

Sentence structure

Spelling

## Hit hard; hit fast.
## Don't cool off until the whole book's cast.

Fly like Jonathan Livingston Seagull. Great thoughts are like great people and follow the rule of James 4:14; they appear like a great cloud in a blue sky---then vanish. They will vaporize before you capture them on paper if you keep on thinking about other details such as: "Did I express that correctly?" "Where is the q key?" Or, "How should I spell...?"

The words, "slow" and "confused" are parasitic partners. It's more difficult to create meaningful copy when you write slowly. How can you relate Chapter 12 to Chapter 3 when you wrote them three weeks apart?

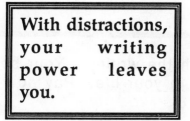

**With distractions, your writing power leaves you.**

WRITER'S POWER

DISTRACTION
DRAIN

In Book II of this series, we'll show you exactly how to speed when you hit the keyboard. Of course, you can't speed unless you have a well organized and paved track to speed on. That's what this book is about.

Like a race horse on its way to your book's finish line, **let nothing distract you..** Every time the phone or door bell rings, you'll lose momentum and your broken concentration will cause product defect. How much?

```
The  more  distractions  you  allow  to
draw  you  away  while  writing  your
first  rough  draft---the  more  tedious
polishing  will  be  required  after  you
finish.
```

Stick with the writing. Your book demands top attention in your life. Pay now or pay a lot more later.

More than anything else, you need to master the art of high speed production when you write. You'll see the task as simple, easy to perform and produce super copy created with 100% of your ability. You'll beat your competition and sell your book while the market for your subject is still hot.

*Text here in Geneva 12 pt.*

> Put two cooks in a restaurant kitchen to prepare a meal. By the time they finish debating about how much spice to add, the customers go somewhere else to eat.

## Chapter 2

# SHOULD YOU CO-AUTHOR OR WRITE ALONE?

Go it alone.

The end.

Writing is like solitary confinement if you work alone. The computer never talks back to you. Since solitary is applied as a severe penalty in prisons, and you're probably a normal, gregarious person, co-authoring might appeal to you.

Some people think two authors can work faster than one, but the real benefit in pairing authors isn't speed. As a matter of fact, two authors collaborating on one book often spend the same time it would take for one of them to write three. In my own attempts, I didn't have too much of the two-cooks-in-the-kitchen problem, but I had to wait to get time before I could meet with him and then proceed. I lost and wasted a lot of time. Goal frustration bothered me.

Still, though, the need for a co-author could be compulsive. If you're anything like I am, you went through life picking up rejection, experiencing failures and criticism. So trying anything new is risky. Do we really know our subject well enough to write about it? Will we look like lonesome jerks if our book fails, or do we need a scapegoat?

Perhaps you feel differently about people than I. Maybe you enjoy working with others. Writing doesn't have to be the world's loneliest task; think about a co-author.

Good reasons for co-authoring are:
1. Somebody else knows more about the subject than you.
2. Better yet, you both know a lot, but the other guy works in the field you will write about and he's known for his knowledge. Therefore, he has clout, which converts to hype—-then sales.
3. You don't get-up-and-go any better than my @#$% lawn mower, so nothing happens until the other writer shows up and yells, "Hey. . ."
4. You don't want to self-publish, and the other guy is already plugged into an agent or publisher.
5. The other writer is established in a writing field (perhaps Hollywood screenwriting) and you offer a percentage to work as an apprentice. Find someone who believes you can produce and sgreer to pay a percentage. Then work diligently to produce a product you can sell with his connections. As you might have heard, it's extremely difficult to get your manuscripts read in Hollywood. I considered speculating on an original film script and wrote once to a manuscript consultant. He wrote the script for *Jaws II*, (Searles) and he was very knowledgeable. His advice: "Forget it." Hollywood is a mean place to work. (Read *ADVENTURES IN THE SCREEN TRADE*, William Golden.)

6. You want to write fiction, and it's great to bounce character integrity and scenarios between you. Group dynamics will often generate dynamic fiction. This is probably the most valid reason for collaborating. Take a look at the movie, *City Slickers*. Ganz and Mandell did a terrific job.

Assuming you want to co-author, you have three things to do:

A. **Pick a person of good character** with whom to write. Prideful people can create miserable work conditions.

B. Settle all the issues in the beginning.

C. Draft a legal contract between the two of you, reduce it to a formal writing, and sign each other's copy.

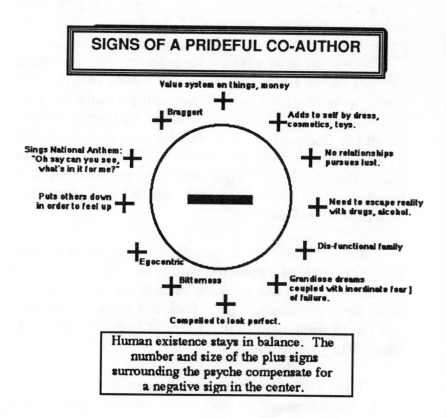

## SIGNS OF A PRIDEFUL CO-AUTHOR

Value system on things, money

Braggert

Adds to self by dress, cosmetics, toys.

Sings National Anthem: "Oh say can you see, what's in it for me?"

No relationships pursues lust.

Puts others down in order to feel up

Need to escape reality with drugs, alcohol.

Dis-functional family

Egocentric

Bitterness

Grandiose dreams coupled with inordinate fear ] of failure.

Compelled to look perfect.

Human existence stays in balance. The number and size of the plus signs surrounding the psyche compensate for a negative sign in the center.

With whom should you write? First, pick a person of principle. Low charactered people are often difficult to deal with. Pairing with a less learned, lazy partner will stifle your creative energies. That's not the best, but it's okay. Pairing with a person of pride and low character will make it nearly impossible to produce a book.

Lots of reasons exist for choosing a person with high moral fiber, but the biggest is this: People of low moral character constantly and compulsively need to inflate their own egos. They are easily offended and frequently FEEL offended, even though no wrong has been done to them. Try to correct THEIR writing and the pain they feel so personally will kill them. On the other hand, they'll slaughter your writing with vengeful compulsion.

When you write a book with anybody, count on putting out 75% of the effort. If you are not willing to GIVE that much, write alone. Any co-author will probably see your efforts through the window of his mind. Self image controls the size of that window. It opens fully only when he reflects on HIS effort, because his self image demands that it open wide. Thus, the battle, "I did more than you," isn't realistic, but often a compulsion to gather-to-self and thus compensate for a negative self image.

Along with that line of thought, it's better not to co-write with someone in authority over you. Bosses can be overbearing. You end up doing most of the work and they make most of decisions. If the book is a winner, your boss will say, "I wrote most of it." But, if it loses, "Something is wrong with your writing style."

If you try co-authoring, you'll learn this: two writers might agree on very little. You'll probably experience disagreement down the writing road. As with most modern marrieds, a power struggle ensues. Ego-hungry partners are only too eager to transform a power struggle over "principle" into a personal war. Therefore, once you've decided to co-author, settle some issues.

Settle on who will have the last word with regard to writing subject matter, style, graphics, page layout, quotes, humor, photos, aphorisms, expertise, plot, etc. Designate one person to be responsible for expenses and the accounting. More important, how will profits be split? Once settled, manage your own responsibilities and don't interfere with your partner's.

What business entity will you use? Partnerships are a bad idea because one partner's debts and mistakes can become the other's. Don't incorporate. You wind up paying double taxes on profits, and the corporate shield from liability doesn't operate, because the First Amendment protects writers well. A limited partnership is not a bad idea, as long as you agree to let one party handle the business aspects of the venture.

Make sure your co-author will have time for the project. You need not only to write your own stuff, but you have to co-relate it to your partner's. So, you write yours, read his, then rewrite both.

I once co-authored a book with somebody who handed me garbage in the beginning (caps and punctuation missing is okay, but random, disorganized thoughts are worse than nothing), so I had to pull apart his mess and try to reorganize it. Even as the project neared completion, the manuscript contained notes such as, "Tell Billy's story." He alone knew what that notation meant, and his super-busy schedule kept us from getting together so he could explain it.

Write up your agreement. Include not only income allocation, but list each partner's responsibilities. Early in your association, you'll develop an outline. Get together, and put it in order. Assign the work evenly. If you fail to do that, the book will wander all over the place. Fiction is an exception to that rule, because the two of you will co-create dynamically. Bouncing off one another can often generate ideas, and the two of you will fill holes in the plot or dialogue easily.

Once in order, write the name of each person responsible for each segment of writing. When you write the contract, attach the writing assignments on the outline. If you write the contract yourself without help from an attorney, just say what you mean, and write what you say. Most legal libraries contain contract forms for partnerships you can excerpt from. KISS; keep it simple, stupid. Don't write anything which either of you might not understand.

My experienced opinion is this: it's best to write alone. I get offers frequently from people who would like to write books, but my co-authoring hasn't made any money.

Here's my advice: **GO IT ALONE.**

THE ~~END~~ BEGINNING.

*Times 12 pt.*

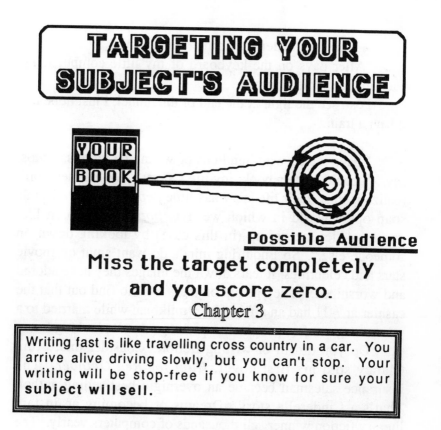

# TARGETING YOUR SUBJECT'S AUDIENCE

**Possible Audience**

## Miss the target completely and you score zero.

Chapter 3

> Writing fast is like travelling cross country in a car. You arrive alive driving slowly, but you can't stop. Your writing will be stop-free if you know for sure your **subject will sell.**

## PICKING THE PERFECT SUBJECT

More writers quit writing for this reason than any other: they lose their sense of self esteem, therefore their ability to produce good copy flattens like a tire. What is it that keeps self esteem pumped? <u>Book sales</u>. But you'll never sell big quantities of books unless you choose a popular subject. How do you do that? Very carefully.

Subject choice is most important. Hesitate. Be careful. **Don't just start writing.** Once you think about a subject you can write about, the urge to write may overpower you. When I wrote *24+ Ways to Use Your Hammock In the Field,* it didn't make a million. Why? My subject matter was not popular.

23

A Country Western performer might sing,
"After days on the keyboard of my little computer, I'm back in the saddle again;
I can see the light at the end of the tunnel, I just hope that it isn't a train."

I have talked with hundreds of wanna-be writers. Most say, "I could write a book; my life's story..." What they don't realize is this: their life story has little *popular* appeal. In this soap-opera world in which we live, *popular* is much like gossip—-"let me get up (in this case) by looking down on someone else." So Enquiring minds <u>do</u> want smut on movie stars and celebrities; it tears down the images they have adored and worshiped. They get up on that. But, to find out that the cashier at 7-11 had an affair with a milkman while married to a salesman gives few people the up-charge they're looking for.

Do you dream of writing fiction? Consider this: Tom Clancy sold his first novel, *Hunt for Red October.* The insurance salesman became an overnight best-selling author. That's a Cinderella story. Dreams of becoming an instant literary fiction winner sell thousands of computers yearly. The same dream also keeps Nevada crap tables full of hopefuls. But the real deal goes like this: Most publishers now let it be known that **you** have to be **known** in order to sell fiction.

Still, your fiction may sell. But just like Clancy, if you want to keep earning, you have to keep writing. Good story-tellers abound, and their popularity is like a flash flood.

So, if it's money you're after, write something other than fiction. I myself would like to write a great novel, but I keep writing "how-to" because I want income twenty years from now. The books I've written to date are my retirement program. We've now sold over 25,000 copies of *COMPASS.*

> **Why not try non-fictiont for a start? It takes less time to write and sells for a lot longer period.**

To succeed in writing, answer this question correctly, "How can you tickle each and every reader's fancy?" In money talk, "What will they buy?" You want your book to sell. It is sad to say, but the cold, hard fact is that we measure success by number of sales.

Examine the science of economics with me and you'll discover the key to sales. The whole thing revolves around supply and demand. Would you like to write a successful book? Write one on a subject for which knowledge is in <u>zero supply</u>, and for which the <u>demand</u> is <u>tremendous</u>. In other words, try to write about something only you know, and lots of other people would like to know. Take your unique experience, position, or knowledge, and market it.

In *EVERYBODY'S KNIFE BIBLE* I did that, and we keep on selling. Likewise, zero supply existed on a lot of the latest outdoor systems we keep re-printing at Path Finder. Our compass course is in the 6th edition. When it comes to not getting lost anywhere without using a map, or using your hunting knife for crucial outdoor measurement, we're the only game in town. Moreover, a lot of people want and **need** to know the exact information we publish. As our country slides downhill, that information is growing in popularity.

Of course, we always get ideas—more than we have time for. This book has been one of them for over a year. We constantly examine new writing ideas, and we'll show you just how we determine if a given project is a "go." Some of the items on the back burners of our production stove contain:

Speed Spanish for Gringos / Total fluency in 27 days.
A religious book about relationships.
Tactical Tennis, two textbooks plus a playbook.
Survival reloading—a lot of material about guns.
A video tape on outdoor life.

No matter what you choose to write, try and be first with the most. See, the money belongs to the pioneers. The basic maxim for financial success is—and always has been—find a need and fill it. In the case of Speed Spanish, the topic is old, but not worn out. New potential customers come into existence every day. We won't produce "yet another..." Ours will be totally different and guarantee the quickest road to fluency. Can we out-distance the competition? We think we can. At least we're convinced enough to gamble $5,000 on the potential return of $30,000.

Maybe your expertise will be in high demand. Ask yourself two basic questions:
A. What do I know about, or, what could I learn about well enough to write a book?
B. Do hordes of people want to know this now, or, will they want to know in the near future?
The answer to B comes in part from analyzing the buying habits of the public. Find out by checking the magazine circulation in *Writer's Market*.

Generally, people buy things for one of three basic reasons: Pride, Profit or Pleasure. Which do you think is most important? The correct answer is Pride, and the capital P is no typo. If what you know will be pridefully demanded by a buying public, start looking for your condo in Monaco.

Target your reading audience, and slant your material to their pride and pleasure. That's why our Green Beret books continue to sell. If you want to live well outdoors, you need us. Besides, we write to entertain. We custom tailor humor for our target audience and mold the comedy into the text. Result: We're fun to read.

Take a walk through a mall. What's selling? T-Shirts. Why not write a design book about good tee-shirts—just good humor? Discount your book to sell with shirts. Get a major shirt manufacturer to distribute for you.

Clothes. Write on how to dress fashionably on a low budget. You get department stores to order advance copies, which they sell at a discount with a clothing purchase.

Foreign. Over two million tourists fly South every year. Could you hire a translator to review local material and write a local guide book? In Costa Rica, for example, only one guide book exists, and it sells well. You can hire an English speaking local for about $200 per month. Hotel information is available over the phone. History is simple.

Sporting Goods. Do you know a sport well? How about an explanation of the different shoes and.the requirements for different uses. Get Nike to back you and sell huge quantities of books to them at a discount.

Satisfy the supply/demand formula, and success will be yours. Potential popularity is your best guide. However, temper that key factor though by sticking to subjects you either know or can learn about easily.

In any publications media—print, audio, or audio visual, the big question is and always has been: **"what will <u>sell</u>?"** If you read William Goldman's *Adventures in the Screen Trade,* you know the answer. So why did the best pros in the movie business lose 35 million dollars on the movie, *Heaven's Gate*? Because the answer to the big question is this: **"Nobody knows."**

Nevertheless, some indicators will give you a hint. Look at the best seller's list for the past six months, and learn what people are reading. More than that, take a look at magazines. Examine their circulation figures in an old *Writer's Market* .Learn what's popular by totaling the number of readers who buy magazines about any given subject. *Outdoor Life Magazine*, for example, circulates a million and a half. Calculate. If you can sell a book to 10% of Outdoor Life readers, you'll earn 150,000 times the net profit on your book. Even at a few dollars each, you could pull in $500,000.

When I wrote *EVERYBODY'S KNIFE BIBLE*. I totalled up more than 3 million readers for outdoor magazines, military magazines and the forestry, camping, and backpacking magazines, because everybody who reads those periodicals uses a knife. You guessed it. We charged ahead with the project. Likewise, we thought our *Hammock Book* would sell to the same audience. We pulled the same trigger one more time, with feeling.

I've lived outdoors and used my knives and hammocks quite a bit, so I thought, "With a little more research, I could learn enough to  produce an outdoor 'how-to' winner." I checked *Books in Print* to make sure nobody else had written a book on my chosen subject. Competition is okay, but the heavy gold goes to those who write exclusives.

In another subject, my children and I discovered enough new information about tennis tactics to write a book. Tennis books appear to be popular as we look in the bookstores, but two tennis magazines circulate less than a million.

I'd studied tennis under Pancho Segura, the great one, while I lived at La Costa. I'd studied tactics while in the Army. Not only that, but we discovered tennis is only taught on a "make yourself play better" basis. Our approach was unique. We keyed off Erma Bombeck's great religious efforts on the subject of being overweight when she prayed something like...

```
"Dear Lord, if you won't help me get thin,
could you please make all my friends get
fat?"
```

If Erma could pray, so could we: "Dear Lord, if you won't help us play better, could you please make all our friends play worse?" We focus on teaching you how to make the other side play worse. With this new approach, the book might take off and fly.

But what will you write about? How old are you? Have you been around and lived an active mental life, or have you passively fed yourself through audio-visual media. Do you have a wide variety of choices?

I write outdoor how-to books for many reasons. I know the subject matter, I enjoy the research, I feel at home with my readers, and I like spending time with other experts.

Inventory your past and make a list. If you have lived awhile and done something besides watch TV, you have some area of expertise gleaned from experience. Where have you been? What have you seen and done? If you have something interesting to teach or appealing to relate, start considering those subjects. Maybe you know someone you can write about, or maybe you have a distant relative who knows someone famous. Whatever your expertise, whomever you know, or wherever you have been, somebody else may want to read about it. Make a list and consider the possibilities. Then make sure you write about your best selling subject first.

> My ex-wife could have made a living writing; she spent a lot of time writing *Bounced Checks.*, *a history of uncontrolled greed.*

She always explained, "I'm not overdrawn; you're under-deposited." We can laugh at that, but, her explanation really holds true for any writer. Do you have to be old to draw from your experience bank? Many say it takes 40 years before you bank enough experience and deposit enough knowledge to keep your books from bouncing like one of my ex-wife's checks.

Basically, once your list is compiled, consider how difficult each will be to complete. Once I owned a computer retail store where I learned a lot about computers. I thought I could produce something useful for the trade, but when I developed the outline, I saw long hours of tedious research ahead. Thus, that product is on the back burner.

If you'll have to spend hours in research to fill out your book, you'll either have to love research or be addicted to your subject. Otherwise, your manuscript will expose your mediocrity. My pastor taught me: Attitudes and thoughts will always control thoughts and actions. Without confidence-generated enthusiasm, your writing will lack luster. Worse, your after-publication enthusiasm will wane and your sales efforts and promotional interviews will likewise flop.

Write to a specific audience and sell through the outlets that support their (sports, hobby) habit. If you can, you want to be the only apple cart in the neighborhood. Bookstores feature your writing in the midst of other authors' writing. Shelf space is scarce. Why compete?

To help you understand more about sales, I should tell you about Dan Poynter. I call him the "Czar of Small Publishers," so a short history is in order. Dan first wrote a book on parachuting. That's a subject of rather narrow popularity. Nevertheless, he sold 170,000 copies. To me, he is the authority on self publishing. I wouldn't even consider writing without owning his great reference, The Self-Publishing Manual. He infrequently conducts seminars in his home (805-968-7277) for only sixteen people (I finally got into one) and points out, "Book stores are lousy places to sell books."

I quite agree. You will too. Wait 'til a few independents who don't pay their bill---even after you spend the cost of the book trying to collect. If you write for money, you're better off to skirt the whole book sales establishment. Face it—manuscripts, and the books they become, are a glut on the market. Reader's Digest used to receive as many as 12,000 submissions a day. If you run a race with thousands of other writers, will you be noticed---much less sold?

So, consider marketing somewhere else. For example, our outdoor books sell through Army/Navy and surplus stores. The customers buy outdoor gear in quantity there, and only a few other books are sold. You can't get much more exclusive. To reach back-packers, campers, hikers and gun enthusiasts, we now produce a sportsman's version with a new cover.

Also, think about adding to your reading audience. Broaden your appeal. In the fourth edition of our compass book, we adapted the system to off-road vehicles, boat and scuba diver use. Including them in the book provided new appeal to a broader audience, so sales increased. You can do the same. Consider **all** the possible interest groups who could use your information. Then write to a broader field to pump sales and popularity as soon as you publish.

Probably, your creative mind will come up with a wide variety of subjects you can write about. Sooner or later you will have to make a final choice. Even if you are the world's finest writer and you draw the best illustrations ever, your book won't fly with an unpopular subject.

With a good subject, however, you'll enjoy sales in the thousands. You may have mistakes in your book, second class illustrations, or an incoherent presentation. But if your subject matter is in short supply and the demand is high, you'll enjoy fortune as your book enjoys fame.

*Main text in 12 pt Times.*

To write fast, you need tools. To make money for tools, you need to sell. To sell---your first book has to be the best you can produce.

## Chapter 4

## TO MARKET FIRST
## WITH YOUR BEST MONEY-MAKER

When you first start writing, you'll probably think about a new project every month or so. After you write more, learn from experience, attend seminars, and study written material---your creative ability will improve. New ideas will pop into your head more often.

Once you've been writing for a while, you'll think up more projects than you'll ever have time to write about. The problem is: which writing to work on first so you make money.

What's the solution? Bring your best and brightest to the front burner. To do this right you need to apply a lot of criteria to your work. If you construct a chart about each product you think of, you'll see immediately how much work and time are involved, and how much the product might earn.

**The more books you print,
the less each book costs.**

# MAKING THE MOST OF YOUR IDEAS

| Proposed Product | Sales Market | Sales Potential in Units | Personal Labor Estimate (Hours) | | Contract Labor Estimate | Product Production Cost |
|---|---|---|---|---|---|---|
| | Video Rental Houses | 10,000 | Research | 0 | | |
| Video for Green Beret Series | Mail Order Retail | 3,000 | Write | 80 | | $5 per unit, small numbers |
| | | | ~~Scrub~~ Rewrite | | | |
| | | | Photo | 8 → | 80 | |
| | | | Shoot | 6 → | $300 | |
| | Established Dealer Outlets | 1,000 | Draw | 12 → | 60 | |
| | | 14,000 | ~~Collate~~ Edit → | | $800 | |
| | | | ~~Cover~~ | | | |
| | | | ~~Design~~ | | | |
| | Computer Factory | | Research | 15 | | |
| B-53 How to write Book in 53 Days | Software Companies | 12,000+ | Write | 85 | | |
| | | | Scrub | 8 | | |
| | | 50,000 | Photo | 8 → | $80 | $7,800 cash |
| | Add-on Producers | | Draw | 35 | | |
| | | 6,000 | Collate | 18 → | $180 | |
| | Copy Shops | 78,000 | Cover Design | 20 → | $200 | |
| | Hammock Factory | 20,000 | Research | 90 | | |
| | | | Write | 28 | | |
| | | | Scrub | 12 | | |
| Hammock 24 ways to use one | Army Surplus | 5,000 | Photo | 26 → | $260 | $2,800 Cash |
| | | | Draw | 8 → | 80 | |
| | Retail Market | 3,000 | Collate | 4 → | 40 | |
| | | | Cover | 6 → | 60 | |
| | Boy Scout | 2,000 | Design | | | |
| | | 30,000 | ~~Research~~ | | | |
| | Foreign Gift Shops! | | Write | 120 | | |
| Speed Spanish for Gringos | | 3,000 | Scrub | 40 | | |
| | | | ~~Photo~~ | | | $8,400 Cash |
| | | | Draw | 35 | | |
| | Retail Market | 1,000 | Collate | 30 | by computer | |
| | | 4,000 | Cover | 2 | $525 | |
| | | | Design | | | |

If you're writing to make money, you want to go with a project that will cost the least and make the most. If you're short of money, you may not be able to print a sufficient quantity of books to come out with a low product cost.

But the gamble factor is tremendous. You may write something you have trouble selling. Should that happen, you may become discouraged in your sales efforts and wind up with a lot of money sitting in your garage.

Think too about dead time. How long will it take from the time you draft the outline until the product hits the stores?

With charts, you no longer have to guess. Your estimates can be sharper, and once you have valid figures in every column, you'll be working on your most productive project.

To know for sure you're on the right track, you have to separate conjecture from fact. Do that carefully. Writers are known for fantasy. That often puts life into a manuscript, but it's death if you don't see market potential with objectivity.

Of course, when you first fill the chart out, you don't know. Don't begin product development until you do know for sure. Be extremely careful when you project sales. Sales times profit will answer the great Shakespearean question: "To write, or not to write." Look, for example, at our hammock book. I figured 10,000 sales to manufacturer(s). I was so sure this product would fly I never checked this out. Besides I couldn't sell a hammock manufacturer what I couldn't show. Since the project was small, I let it fly anyway.

What if they wouldn't buy? I had an ace up my sleeve. Copyright on the book was already mine so all I would have to do is find a cheap source for hammocks (probably from the

Philippines) to sell with my book. That way, I would have a package to offer better than any other hammock vendor, and Path Finder is established in the sporting goods world anyway. Any customer who bought my hammocks would automatically get a bonus——a book on how to use it to make him king of the woods.

Maybe whatever you write first should be a video? In addition to thinking about sales, think about initial investment. Look at the cost of video. Up front we pay a little more for development of the master copy, but after that, we need only to build enough product to satisfy immediate demand. Video tapes cost production money, but the ratio of "profit to cost" is much better and the demand is high. Audio cassette tapes also require less initial investment than books, because you reproduce a few at a time. Calendars and postcards are cheaper yet.

Prioritize. Try and attain product development and production at a low cost——then sell millions. But even with the chart helping you to plan, another unwritten rule has a big influence on what you write. *Work on the project which is closest to producing sales and money.*

Why? A. As any project nears completion, you may get the jitters. Rejection and failure loom at you like something on the order of a huge truck travelling toward you——in your lane. Nobody wants to fail. What if your writing doesn't find popular acceptance? Will this book die? ...and take you under the ground with it? If it's close to done, do it.

B. The income from sales on a finished product will support you while you work on a new one.

Many writers try to avoid death with this self-deceptive ploy: "Yeah, I am almost finished; I just have it stored on disc for a while so I can take an objective look at it." Sure. . .

Don't do that; face the firing squad. If what you wrote fails and you live through the experience, your next product will improve depending on how constructively you apply the lessons of failure.

I thought I could knock this book out in a hurry. When I didn't see many other how-to's on speed writing around, I was further encouraged. Perhaps, a book teaching writers how to produce quick manuscripts will sell. We'll see. In the writing game, you're either famous by Friday or morose the Monday after.

If you are anything like me, your mind flits from one thought to another faster than a New York minute. Save time, money, and mis-directed effort. Put a chart together so all of your planned projects make dollars and sense.

Match the project's cost against your ability to pay for it. Then, carefully analyze the potential earnings. Take a long look at how much of your own development time will be involved. When you plot all these factors, you'll create a stress free work atmosphere for yourself. Then, after you have a steady income from your first effort, you can take all the time in the world to come up with a blockbuster.

*Times in 12 pt.*

| PROJECT NAME | KIND | COMPLETION TIME | COSTS Develop/ Produce | SALES QUANTITY | UNIT PROFIT | PROFIT TOTAL/Time |
|---|---|---|---|---|---|---|
|  |  |  |  |  |  |  |
|  |  |  |  |  |  |  |
|  |  |  |  |  |  |  |
|  |  |  |  |  |  |  |
|  |  |  |  |  |  |  |
|  |  |  |  |  |  |  |
|  |  |  |  |  |  |  |
|  |  |  |  |  |  |  |

> Winning runners need a strong kick at the end of a race. Quick writers needc the same. To make the final hours of book production pass quickly, smooth out the running course ahead of time. If you don't do that, you'll come to the end of the race and encounter hurdles and obstacles in your way.

## Chapter 5

# THE KEY TO SPEED: ORGANIZING YOUR IDEAS

Situation: You've chosen your subject. You have ideas of your own, and you've learned a lot from research. You discovered some nuggets when you wrote away for information. Some of your material is super. You found some great humor and adapted it to your subject. Most of your subject matter was not in print at this time. (You checked BOOKS IN PRINT.)

## NOW---AGONIZE AND ORGANIZE

Your book could well be a hit. This is the most difficult part of the writing task. It takes concentration plus. Lots of writers bypass it. But take it from me, someone who has never paid attention to detail, and suffered all his life as a result: you MUST stop to organize. A sign over my desk reads:

> **"IF YOU DON'T HAVE TIME TO DO IT RIGHT, HOW WILL YOU EVER FIND TIME TO DO IT OVER AGAIN?"**

A well organized outline prevents writer's block; (see glossary), which, just like heart disease, is much easier prevented than cured. It also makes manuscripting a dream.

Writing is much like swimming in a river. You either struggle upstream, swim normally cross stream, or move like a motorboat down stream. When "what to write next" baffles you, the writing will be difficult, tough going—-an upstream swim. If your chapter outlines are complete, you can cruise down stream as you write.

But, mess up by not organizing before you start, and your first rough draft will have middle information at the beginning, and opener information at the end. I wound up trying to organize my first manuscript after I wrote it by spreading it all over a gymnasium floor. To fix it and get it together, I penciled in the main thought of each paragraph, and then searched for a place where it could match up and flow smoothly in with the others. I had a similar problem when I went ahead and built a house after giving a very loose interpretation to the plans. Both were messes, and both cost me double the time to try and correct and camouflage them.

Incomplete outlining causes your book to go like economic reform in eastern Europe: "You are HUNGARY for money, so you were RUSSIAN to write before you outlined and planned your work, so you never FINNISH."

What's best about good organization is this: It FREES YOUR CONCENTRATION FOCUS. Without that, you'll spray good thoughts and great ideas throughout your manuscript like shotgun pellets most of which go over your readers' heads. Also, you may feed the reader one of your gems in chapter 2 and then re-run it in chapter 17.

Achieving great literary copy is like decking someone in a Karate match. Listen to the words of Sun Duck Sun, the exalted grand master of Korean Tae Kwon Do. He writes, "bring your strength, weight, heart, and mental power to the point of contact." For writers, where might that be? **The current paragraph!**

With no properly progressing and tied-together thought patterns, you meander like a drunk through the streets of your book, and often wind up in a gutter. But, succeed in outlining, and concentration focus is yours. The writing will be easy and fun. With an emancipated mind and spirit, you'll be free to concentrate on adding jokes to your manuscript at exactly the right place, inserting the correct quotes at the right time, and tying the information together so it advances at a beautiful, symphonic pace.

Therefore, work at organization, regardless of the pain. Put your ideas in order. Don't let yourself be distracted. Great segments of prose will flash across your mind and the urge to write them will be overpowering. Don't do as I have! Consider and concentrate only on the book as a whole. Don't let your mind fall into the trap of writing one sentence.

> **EVEN IF YOU WRITE THE MOST CLEVER SENTENCE IN THE WORLD, IT WILL READ LIKE JUNK IF IT DOESN'T FIT IN THE CHAPTER.**

True, you'll get some great ideas at the wrong time. After years of intense study on the subject, I have formulated the writers' LAW OF INSPIRATION:

> **THE BEST IDEAS WILL ALWAYS OCCUR TO A WRITER WHILE IN A PLACE OR ACTIVITY WHICH MAKES IT ABSOLUTELY IMPOSSIBLE TO WRITE THEM DOWN.**

Also, the **Law of Exigent Authorship:**

_urgent, demanding_

---

## THE MORE PRESSING AND SEVERE THE EMERGENCY AT HAND, THE LESS WILL BE YOUR ABILITY TO LOCATE A PEN

---

At first I thought I could remember the great writing ideas that trickled into my mind at the oddest times. I couldn't. Even after I took a memory course, I forgot where I parked my car. Now, though, wherever I go, I carry something to write with. One of my pens has a cord on it so it hangs around my neck. Some of my best thoughts are recorded next to gravy stains on napkins.

As soon as you've decided to write your book, buy index cards and record your inspirations the minute they cross your mind. Later, you can shuffle them into correct order. I keep cards on my boat and truck, in my bathroom, in my Bible, on my bed stand, and in my tennis bag.

You can fill in your cards almost everywhere you go. A hot idea will frequently occur while you're driving back and forth to work, or during leisure. If I write a lot of information on one card, I copy it off on two others. Remember, don't get wordy. Nice, neat, easy-to-read phrases representing different ideas are all you write down.

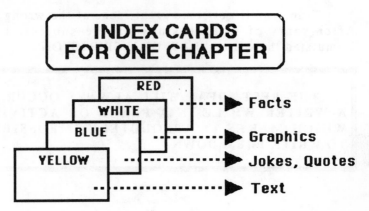

INDEX CARDS FOR ONE CHAPTER

RED ········▶ Facts
WHITE
BLUE ····▶ Graphics
YELLOW ··········▶ Jokes, Quotes
··········▶ Text

Use various color index cards for different material. Illustrations, graphs, drawings and photos can all go on different colors. Text, references, jokes and quotes can likewise be separated. Staple all the cards for each individual chapter together.

While you're adding material for each chapter on the different cards, think priority. With EVERYBODY'S KNIFE BIBLE, I asked myself, "What's the best in this book?" Thus, I moved "Converting your knife into a super Green Beret woods tool" to the front. Because of that, we drew great reviews from editors with time to read only one chapter.

### THE SCRATCH OUTLINE (Scratch.otl)

Your scratch outline contains only the chapter titles. Once you have everything on your index cards, don't copy it all on your screen. First, just copy the chapter titles and headings. Remember, you want zip in your script and pizazz in your chapter titles.

MOVING YOUR BEST
CHAPTER UP
NEAR THE FRONT
OF YOUR BOOK

The scratch outline (compufile name: Scratch.otl) is invaluable for organizing because it's the skeleton of your book. Like a department store mannequin, you drape and re-arrange a great variety of colorful and persuasive thought on it.

The desire to organize any outline quickly and well can make you fall in love with your computer software. Instead of penned scratch-outs, lines all over the place, scissors and glue, you push buttons and your ideas move into proper order as if by magic.

Any word processor will do the job for you. Special outline softwares all work pretty much the same. First, designate the text you want to move, (we also call this "clamshelling"). Next, position the cursor at the new location and, voila, tell the computer to move the designated (blocked) text there. Macs are different. Sure, you block, and it's easier, but then you move the block to a storage area called a clipboard with a {cut} command. (Point and click.) To get it back where you want it, point and click on {paste}.

Remember---the brackets or parenthesis we use to surround computer commands will tell you which computer we refer to.

WORD PERFECT COMMANDS: < >.
WORDSTAR COMMANDS: [ ].
MAC COMMANDS: { }.

The brackets only set the commands apart from text. For any command using an IBM clone we use the ^ to designate the control key. For the MACINTOSH, we write Apple to mean the key which most approximates "#" as well as the apple sign (on most keyboards).

Command your word processor to make an extra copy of your outline. In WordStar, block top [^KB] and bottom [^KK] of the part you want to duplicate. Use [^KC] to make an extra copy, and then write the blocked file [^KW] onto the disk. Name it differently.

Once you have two scratch.otl files, rename one of them "Contents." Name it the same way on the Mac. On the desk top screen, click on the subject icon or file designation, and tell the Mac on a pull down menu to make a copy {Apple D}.

Back on IBM, use the file labeled contents to build your outline. With Insert-on, [^V], expand the original file by typing in all the notes from your index cards. Major ideas protrude left; minor ideas should appear indented more to the right. Most of the advanced word processors today have outline features. You'll have an easy time moving text and setting various indents to indicate idea strength.

After all the information for each chapter is into your computer, print out. Look at the amount of material you have for each chapter. Then make a good estimate of the number of pages each chapter will contain. Total up your page estimates for all chapters combined. To fill the signatures at the printing company, target your text for 10-14 pages less than a signature multiple.

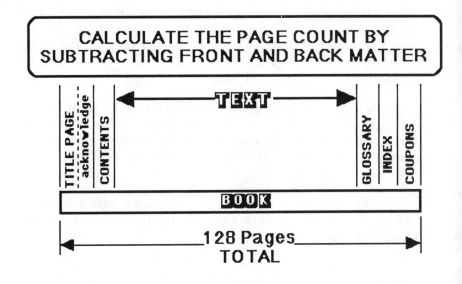

You're going to produce a multiple of 32 pages because printers use plates called signatures, each containing that number. When you deliver camera ready copy to fill out the printer's drum capacity, you get the most printed pages for the same low price. Plan to write between six to twelve pages in each chapter. Thus you'll be shooting for twelve to sixteen chapters. Of course, each chapter you write must be an EVEN number of pages. That's because every chapter will start on an ODD, FACING page.

So, 4 X 32 = 128, and 5 X 32 = 160, which means you will write a total of either either 118 or 148 pages of text. The other dozen or so pages will contain:

Four pages at the front of the book:
Title                    1
Copyright page      1
Table of contents    2
Total          =     4
Six pages appear at the back of the book:
Index                2
Glossary           2
Order Coupons      4
Total          =     6

Of course, the longer your book, the longer the index and glossary. So you could use more than the ten page allotment. Since we have other titles, we use more coupon pages. You'll be making final adjustments to text during the final collate.

When you assign a "compufile" title to each chapter of your outline, use the first space(s) for the chapter's number, so you can locate a chapter easily on your screen. Start with 100; that way all your files stay in order.

The Mac does a lot better. You can pull a window down and click your mouse so it lists your files by alphabet, date or size.

Some of my outlines were the best in the world, I thought. But when I returned to them, they screamed for help. Yours will, too. Just save it [^KD] onto your disc, and forget it for a few days. When you come back to it, you'll have fresh ideas.

While your outline is resting on a computer disc, use the time. Gather more information and do some research. Mix in new ideas, subject-related humor.

## ORGANIZING ILLUSTRATIONS
Think through the project graphically (see Chapter 13). For now, figure out where your illustrations may go. Rough sketches on an index card with the proper chapter number help you build a list of illustrations as you write. You type out the picture in words, (see A. below), then block that text and record it to the illustrations file.

If you work on a Mac, read through your test and sketch on a graphics program. (I use SuperPaint.) Make a folder for each chapter of text you write, and label it with the chapter number and a chapter heading abbreviation (about 8 letters). Put the drawings in each chapter. Also, put the titles for each photo in the folder.

You may think graphically, so draw first; write later. I don't draw very well, so even though SuperPaint helps a lot, I write first, then print out and draw for each chapter later. Draw your illustrations once; save and forget about them for a few days. Later, re-edit your drawings to get the best results. The more you go over your illustrations, the better they'll communicate.

To write as well as you possibly can, fill your outline with more information than you need. Later, just before you start the actual writing of the book, use various colored highlighter pens to mark off the more important items in each chapter outline. Dark green is the color I use if the material doesn't fit in a chapter well. Red colors the material which best goes to the front or could work in the cover presentation. Yellow designates fair, and blue is for material you think is best.

Check your filled in outline carefully. Look for weak material or stuff that doesn't quite fit. Color code it for replacement, even if you don't have anything now to replace it with. God may inspire you with better material, or you can leave it out altogether if you have to size a chapter down.

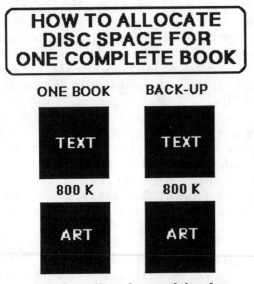

## HOW TO ALLOCATE DISC SPACE FOR ONE COMPLETE BOOK

ONE BOOK      BACK-UP

TEXT      TEXT

800 K      800 K

ART      ART

Use two discs for each book.
One is for art, the other for text.
The extra two discs are back-ups.

Pull out four 3.5 inch floppy discs, each holding 720K on a PC or 800K on a Mac. Dedicate one disc for writing text, and a duplicate to record your newest effort every day. Record the latest update on your back-up disc's label. Put all your artwork on another, and likewise, make a back-up.

Now, you have a scratch outline, a completely filled-in outline, and a list of illustrations. Your discs are lined up, labeled, and ready to store your book and artwork. Where else can you go but up, up and away!

Take a break; enjoy some research. That's next.

*This chapter was printed in NEW YORK 10 pt.*

## BENEFITS FROM ADDED RESEARCH

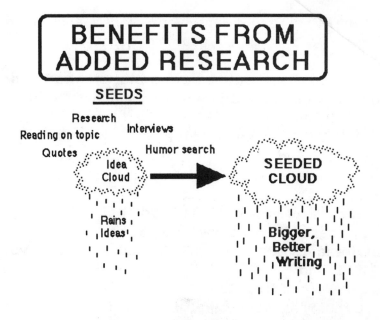

SEEDS

Research
Reading on topic
Quotes
Interviews
Humor search

Idea Cloud

Rains Ideas

SEEDED CLOUD

Bigger, Better Writing

Chapter 6

## TAKE A BREAK
## ENJOY THE JOY OF RESEARCH

Why research? To produce quick manuscript copy, you need confidence. When you know (almost) all there is to know about your subject matter, you can fly through manuscript creation. You won't have to stop and think about what goes where next. Moreover, you won't have to steach out your writing with flimsy material.

You want to be the best you can, so find out more than "all there is to know" about your subject. Once you have extra pages of researched material in your outline, you can trash your worst and serve up only your best to your readers.

Of course other reasons might also suggest you dig into your subject with a pick and shovel.

A. You may need filler. If your outline is sparse and you can't reasonably estimate a good page count, you'd better learn a lot more about your subject.

B. You cannot afford to be wrong. Every detail must be accurate; otherwise your readers AND YOUR REVIEWERS will see you as a fraud. Result: you and your entire book lose credibility.

C. Competition will be severe. If your book sells well, I can think of a few dozen writers who will consider a spin-off. How do you prevent this? Cover your subject so well that empty holes are almost non-existent. Thus, competing authors will have a harder time digging into your market.

D. Lack of knowledge is one of the major causes of writer's block. If you don't know, you can't write.

E. Extra knowledge make you feel like an expert when you write, so your text will exude confidence. The same principle makes clothes important. If you look like a million dollars, you'll feel like a million, and therefore act like a million. Your writing will be the same.

If you fail to research, your writing will be like a newborn kitten––very tentative. That's how garbage appears in your writing like, "It would seem as if the best way to go might be.." (Isn't that poor?) No, no, Lone Ranger. Research! Then write: "This is best. ."

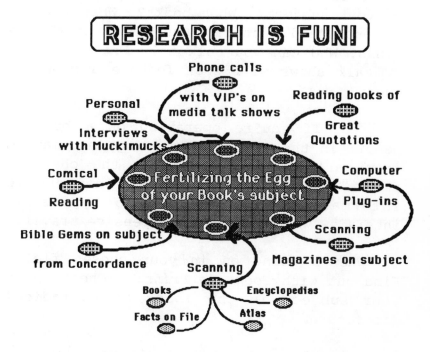

Later on, while doing radio or TV talk shows, you can represent what you wrote with excitement. Believe me, if you don't know for sure that your book is best, when you think and talk about it you'll send a poor message. Lack of confidence or enthusiasm will have a poor effect on sales. If you write without researching and still exude confidence in your text, interviews and post-publication sales, you ought to try acting---there's more money in it.

Study about how to research fully by reading several books on the subject. For now, begin by listing possible sources of information. What magazine articles exist on your subject? What books? What reviews of published matter? Can you access data banks? Who can you talk to? What radio or TV talk shows will soon feature a quotable guest?

If you're operating on a budget, pencil in the cost of acquiring information from various sources and hit the cheapies first. You may get enough inexpensive information to allow you to bypass an interview which requires expensive travel.

What's going on in your chosen field? Find out with *Books in Print*. Check up on your subject in the *Index to Periodical Literature*.

One of my favorite writers, John L. Springer, told me he did this: In New York, he'd make a list of periodicals containing information about his subject. He dropped the list off at his favorite used magazine store. In a couple of hours, a stack of take-home research would be ready for him. A few days after that, he could write about his subject with a newly charged information bank. Call the used book and magazine stores in your area. In Las Vegas, for example, I found some gems.

For the quickest research in the world, hook your computer up to a 1200 or 2400 baud modem. Read Alfred Glossbrenner's fascinating book, *How to Look it up on Line*. He teaches you how to make your computer read over 1,000 magazines—2.38 million paragraphs—in under 25 minutes. Now, that's research!

As the hits (bits of information on the subject you inquired about) come up on your screen, you can save the information to disc and print it out in your office. No gas; no leg work. Moreover, you suffer no disappointment because a book or magazine you needed from the library wasn't there.

> Even though I won't use all of the material I dig up, a lot of it stimulates my creativity.

In addition to using the modem, make personal phone calls. When I wrote *Everybody's Knife Bible*, I inserted a chapter called, "Self defense for women." Since I advocated the use of a two edged (illegal) knife, I called the prosecuting attorney's office and the Rape Crisis Center in Hawaii. I was surprised to learn this: A woman's house may be her castle, but her body has nowhere near that status. Why? Long trials. Prosecutors today are so backed up they can't take a long trial.

In the name of providing a "good" defense, criminal defense lawyers almost always threaten a long trial unless the D.A. deals. Result: plea bargain, and the thugs on the street know they can get away with most anything. Mace was illegal in our 50th State, so I asked about the illegality of women defending themselves with a knife. "Yes," said the prosecutor, "it is illegal, but they'll get away with it easily." Phone calls are the fishing expeditions of research. You have to make a lot of casts, but you get back some interesting fish.

Check the appropriate sections of all the humor books you can find. When writing anything bibliographical, look through all the jokes in the personality attributes sections of the person you're writing about. Was he stingy, a womanizer? Look under those headings. In a collection of jokes under the heading: "books," I recently found this double-entendre:

**HOW WILL YOUR BOOK BE BOUND?**
**WITH GOOD RESEARCH, IT WILL BE BOUND**
**FOR SUCCESS!**

Many writers overlook humor books and famous quotations. But now, since readers accept call-out boxes and side-bars and most publishing softwares provide them in the package, you don't have to flow quotes and humor smoothly into your own writing. The actual research for humor and quotations is simple. You merely look under the headings of the chapter titles in your book. Take time and be deliberate when you do this. It's like searching through an attic. You never know when you'll find something that just fits perfectly.

Check television programming. Hot quotes make your book come alive with authenticity, and TV talk show hosts make millions a year for eliciting incredible remarks from celebrities. Recently, I helped a pastor write *Financial Freedom*, a book about wealth and money attitudes. I caught Richard Pryor saying money was a curse. He said, "I couldn't put my pipe down, and, in disgust, I poured alcohol over myself and lit myself on fire."

Most talk shows will send a transcript for a fee so you can back up your quotes with proof.

Radio shows can be the best ever. Some of Larry King's guests have provided some superbly marketable quotes. Even better, you can talk to the guest. Here's how to capture these for your very own book: Call during the show **early**, stay short and punchy, and ask your question. Let Larry and the guest do the talking. Be gracious. Then let your readers know about it when you write this sensational tid-bit, "when I talked with Arnold Schwarzeneggar over the phone..."

As a result of one such show, I can say I called Sidney Sheldon and asked about breaking into screen writing. He said, "Yes, it's impossible, but newcomers arrive every year." Any good quote adds a little spark to your manuscript, but Sidney Sheldon? Now, that's explosive lightning! **(I didn't say I knew him; I just said I called him.)**

When you quote an authority in the field, your book acquires the clout of that authority. That's why a personal interview is a great idea. Many people are too afraid to talk freely over the phone. You'll encounter this more often if your book deals with sensitive material. So, if you have a hunch there's something golden to acquire, see your source personally. You establish rapport, and the resulting spirit of trust pays handsome dividends with inside information you could never obtain any other way.

To make your writing fact-filled, interesting and authentic, dig for knowledge and background. Dig hard and you'll become confident enough to write like a real authority in your subject field. Add facts to give your book real substance. Add quotes to polish it beyond comparison. Then add humor to entertain your readers. All of that will keep your readers hungry for more.

## Chapter 7

## PANNING YOUR OUTLINE FOR THE GOLD AND SIZING UP YOUR JEWEL FOR QUICK PRODUCTION

Remember when we left your outline hanging? Well, pick it up again; print it out, and look it over. Since you've been digging for gold with your research shovel, you can now dress out your manuscript so it shines. Add additional facts, lively quotes, relative anecdotes, and on-subject humor. Put all those additions and changes into the outline file on your computer.

Now, re-estimate your page count for each chapter. Total the number of all chapter pages to estimate book size.

In every science or method, one technique or trick stands out as THE INSIDE SECRET for doing the job. Here is **THE KEY** to rapid writing:

> **CLAMSHELL EACH CHAPTER IN YOUR OUTLINE SO IT BECOMES AN INDIVIDUAL CHAPTER IN YOUR BOOK—-A SEPARATE FILE OF ITS OWN.**

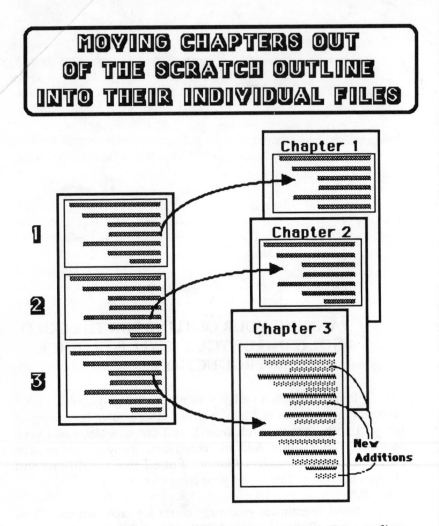

## MOVING CHAPTERS OUT OF THE SCRATCH OUTLINE INTO THEIR INDIVIDUAL FILES

Chapter 1

Chapter 2

Chapter 3

New Additions

If you use a typewriter, use scissors to cut up your outline. Paste each chapter outline on a separate piece of paper to create a bare-bones individual chapter.

On a computer, use a trick called "blocking." It's similar to using a clamshell digger to dig up a portion of your total outline by setting "beginning" and "ending" blocks. Once blocked, or "dug up," you copy the dug-up portion to your disc and give it a separate title of its own. Thus saved, the "dug-up" chapter of your outline becomes a **chapter of your book**, rather than a part of your outline.

Block each successive chapter and write it to disc. Result: Your disc will contain several separate chapters. On your Mac, block by clicking on your mouse and dragging the cursor through the material. Then on a pull down menu, release the mouse button when the arrow highlights {copy}. That moves the copy of the individual chapter portion of your total outline to a storage vault in your computer called "clipboard." Then open a new file with the proper name, and paste from the clipboard into it.

When all chapter parts of your outline have become individual chapters of their own, abandon [^KQ] {click on close box} to save your outline file. Both the Mac and IBM programs will ask you if you want to save as is or as was. Answer no when it asks you, "Save changes?" Don't save the changes to your old outline file. You will want to use both the new files you created as well as the old file you worked from. Print it out again. Among other things, you'll use it for pencilled-in additions and to record **not the estimated, but the real number** of pages, after you write each chapter.

**6      PANNING  .  8**
**Chapter #    Title        pages**

Once the blocking and copying is all complete, each chapter appears on your screen index as a separate file. Each chapter title should contain: a chapter number at the beginning, a name, and your estimated page count.

You should be looking at 16-20 short chapters, all as separate files. If one chapter is long, split it into halves—A & B—to make it easier to work with on the computer. You can rejoin it when you're ready to print. That way, when you rewrite and add more, you won't have to wait for a slow (therefore less expensive) computer to travel a long distance.

Short chapter files make things easier for both human and computer brains to work with. The same advice goes for Mac users as well. Even though MicroSoft Word is very quick, Quark takes time because every change re-arranges the whole manuscript. PageMaker does the same. Remember, use short files.

After you've converted all the chapter segments of your outline to their own book chapters on your disc, expand these individual chapter outlines by adding new material. You want each chapter outline to contain all the information you have. Make absolutely sure all your information appears exactly where it belongs. This is the last shot you take at fixing your outline. The more concentration you apply to this effort now, the faster and easier it will be to produce your manuscript later. On the other hand, fail to be scrupulously neat now and you will pay double or triple later. You'll be blocking and moving material all over the chapters. Confusion may reign and rain.

---

**Confused writers don't write;**
**they falter and brood.**

---

Set up your page size. Cost goes up as you waste paper at the printers. Think about book shelves too. Don't make it hard for the clerks. Remember, most book browsers will pull your book because of what they see on the spine.

Full size books use 8 1/2" by 11" paper. Cut a page like that in half and you'll see what a standard trade paper book looks like. Think about page count. If your book will go over 224 pages, think about publishing two books.

How and where will your book be used? At Path Finder, for example, one of our big hits has been a book which teaches you how never to get lost without using a map. We make it pocket-size so a hiker can carry it easily.

Your book's finished size will be 5 1/2 X 8 1/2. To produce nice looking margins, type 4.3 inches across a page, so you leave a little over a half inch on both sides. I didn't do that with this book right away because I was scared about running over my signature count. For PCer's, if you print out at 12 CPI (characters per inch), set the right margin at [^OR 51 Return].  On a Mac, flow the words and illustrations to make beautiful pages with QuarkXpress or PageMaker.  Quark allows you to play with fonts and leading until you have it exactly the way you want it.  You can adjust fonts and leading to get a good looking 15 CPI, so 64 characters on a line will do just fine.  Remember, you'll enlarge each chapter with graphic illustrations, photos and call-out boxes.

Computer paper has 66 lines.  In WordStar, command your word processor to print out 41 lines with generous margins on the top and bottom of the page.  WordStar employs dot commands to do this.  Make one file called "dotcom" and save that file to disc.  Your dotcom files for WordStar should look like:

.pl66   page length
.mt13   margin, top
.mb12   margin, bottom
.pc25   page # column
.pn ?   page number   (fills in later)

Then, call it in [^KR] at the beginning of every chapter.  When moved to the beginning, those dot commands configure your manuscript to print out in camera ready copy.

A MacIntosh is wonderful.  Both MacWrite II and MicroSoft Word display a similar ruler line and you simply drag icons.  When you finally import to QuarkXpress or PageMaker, you call up the set-up page and plug in your page values.   I use one file for each chapter (about 8 pages without illustration popcorn).  If you go through Micro-Soft Word to get to Quark (as I do), spell check and word count first.  Try 5.5 by 8.5 and see how many pages accept how many words.  Here's a formula to find total text words.

| Word count times total page count equals total words. |
|---|

Will you have to add?  You can draw, photograph, or add quotes and humor in call out boxes so your chapters each end on an EVEN page.  The last thing to do is change your  VIEW to *"fits in window"*  so you can check your manuscript for widows and orphans. Use "section" to re-adjust your page count. Then save.

On IBM, drop down to approximately the sixteenth line of your opening page and type in the "chapter and number." The command, [^OC], <Shift F-6>, {click on "center"} will move it exactly to the center of your page. If the chapter title is over six words long, consider a second, centered line as well. Drop down two more lines and write in the title of the chapter in CAPS. Again, center that. The Mac gives you a choice of font, size, and a variety of letter styles in that font and size such as bold, italic, outlined or shadowed letters. Once you choose, be consistent. All chapter headings should appear in your book in the same font and style. Go with something different from the style you use in the text; set off your chapter titles so they appear to be distinct. For example, if you use a sans-serif font in text, go with a serif for titles.

Tell the computer the correct page number on the beginning page of each chapter. On a Mac in MS Word 4.0, drop the format window down and release-click on {document}. Down in the middle on the left side, look for "Number Pages from ." After you write in the proper number, hit {Apple J}. Thus, your page numbers stay in proper succession as you switch files for a new chapter. If chapter 4's last page is 28, (**always an even number**), chapter 5 begins with page 29 (always an odd number for a facing page at the beginning of each chapter). If you finish a chapter with an odd number of pages, delete text or popcorn it out by adding script or illustration.

After working in the trade for a long time and calculating all the thought processes involved, I have discovered and formulated :

> **Only when the whole book is finished will the idea of changing the chapter order pop into your head.**

Zazhbatt! That's been my experience. If it happens to you, you have to make five different changes. Call up and change the scratch outline, the expanded outline, the Table of Contents, the chapter titles and sub-headings, and the dot commands for page numbering [.PN]. On the Mac, renumber the pages by release-clicking on {Section, then Document} under the Format heading on your screen. If you fail to make each and every one of these changes, you'll be more confused than some of our politicians.

# SOLVING THE PROBLEMS OF A CREATIVE, BUT FRAGMENTED MIND

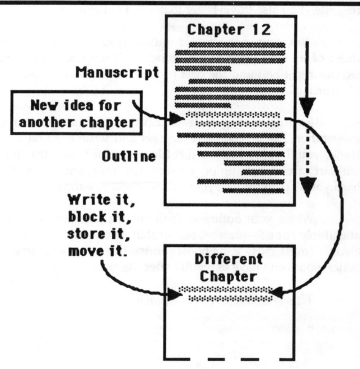

Think of writing as if you were driving a car. Manuscripting a well-outlined book is like driving on a smooth concrete highway. Your computer and brain travel smoothly along. You enjoy the ride as you glide up off-ramps indicated by signs you recognize because you put them there.

The other way to travel is over a rough road, with no signs to guide you, bumps all over, and stretches of highway and parts of bridges missing as if they were in Iraq. The going will be tough; it seems as if you might never reach your destination 128 long, difficult pages away from where you started. Ruts in the road jar your frame and cause your tires to go flat. Even if you arive alive, you'll need lots of repairs and replacements.

Just as with automobiles, repairs often take more time than original fabrication. For every hour you spend smoothing the road by revising your outline, you save between two and three hours in re-write. You also travel faster to the end of the book.

Revising each chapter outline is hard---even more so for those of us who want to get going. Outline smoothing requires tedious repetition and the best concentration you can muster. But it's worth it.

Rapid-writing is like racing. If you spend time in preparation, put all the parts together and write right on a smooth track, you'll enjoy instant throttle response. But, try to get by without careful tune-up on a rough dirt track, and no matter how hard you step on the gas, your dragster will be a drag.

When your outline is finally bolted together, smoothed out and finely tuned—praise God—install safety belts on your office chair. You'll cross your book's finish line in record time. Even better, you won't have to rebuild after the race.

*This chapter in 10 pt. Palatino*

DAY CLOCK FOR BOOK PRODUCTION

BOOK BIRTH!

53! 0

rotates

45 | | 15

DAY CLOCK

30
Days

## Chapter 8

## THE FUN OF RACING
## A 53 DAY CLOCK.

Here's the plan: write 128 pages (minus 12 or so) in 53 days. Possibly, you may overwrite. If you also popcorn the manuscript up with photos and illustrations, you could easily    fill out another signature (32 pp.) But for 128 pages on the first edition, you have to write approximately five per day. . . Correct?   Wrong.

Writing isn't all you do.  You need time to think through the project graphically, and maybe even draw the pictures.  If you're going to shoot pictures, you need to write a schedule of photography for a camera person.

My most productive day yielded twenty-two pages. That day, I never got out of bed; I wrote with my keyboard on my lap. The book was EVERYBODY'S KNIFE BIBLE, and I blasted the first rough draft (no photos, drawings, collating, glossary or index) to completion in two weeks.

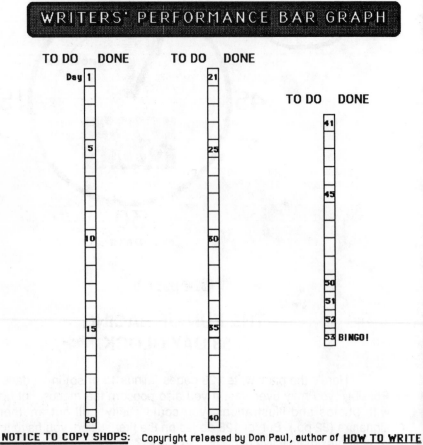

WRITERS' PERFORMANCE BAR GRAPH

TO DO    DONE        TO DO    DONE

Day 1                    21

5                        25

                                    TO DO    DONE

                                    41

10                       30          45

15                       35          50
                                    51
                                    52
20                       40          53 BINGO!

Take this book to a copy shop and enlarge the WRITERS' PERFORMANCE BAR GRAPH. If you can, go 200% twice so you get a wall poster.

Of course, 128 pages in two weeks works out to an average of eleven pages per day. Piece o' cake! Try hard to stay on schedule. Once you start, don't stop. Suffering writer's block is like falling off a horse. If you don't climb back in the saddle immediately, you may never ride again.

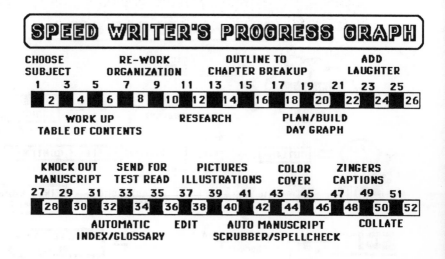

Sure, I bog down. I take showers, (cold) and bike rides. When I am dragging, I even try to lift weights. Poynter takes walks around his Santa Barbara mansion to get his circulation going. No matter what you do, keep on writing. Make your quota.

Allocate just so many days to write your manuscript. All you do is follow your outline. Later, add some humor, develop illustrations, and revise. Remember, you'll do a lot of the tedious production automatically. You have to polish your writing three—maybe four—times, and the Table of Contents a half dozen times.

---

**MAKING YOUR WRITING QUOTA IS YOUR DAILY TASK**
**Don't fail. Look; this pressure will only last a few weeks.**

---

On 128 pages you might install approximately fifty photos and drawings, which means collating could take two full days.

You stay ahead or fall behind depending on each day's performance. If you stay with the plan, however, 53 days later you can take your little manuscript to the printer.

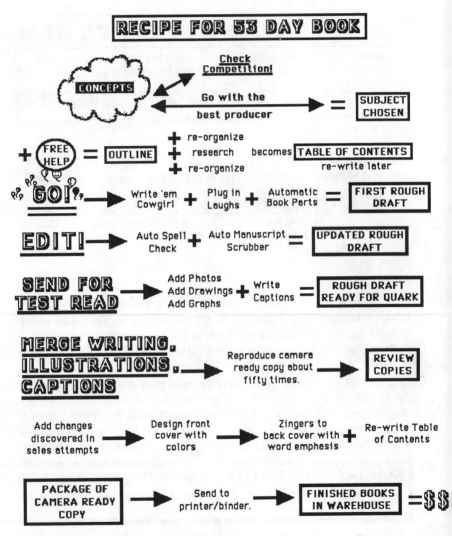

*Maint text done in Helvetica 10 pt.   QUOTA box in Chicago.*

> When you know you write well, you can write a lot faster. To write your best, use the language you've spoken all your life. Then charge your battery so you discover the joy of flying on a keyboard.

## Chapter 9

# SOURCE, MEANING, AND HUGE RESULTS FROM POWER WRITING

> ### Writing books is like writing checks.
> A book either enriches or bounces depending entirely on what the writer has available in his brain-bank. Write books nobody can read and you'll be consistent when you write checks nobody can cash.

Some authors overdraw their book writing account. The riches were there, but they tried to deliver more than they had. So, their book bounces. Others under-deposit. They write blindly the way people write checks before payday—and hope whatever they write clears into the reader's brain. Whether you overdraw or under-deposit, the result is the same: you wrote a rubber book. Rather than enrich, it bounces.

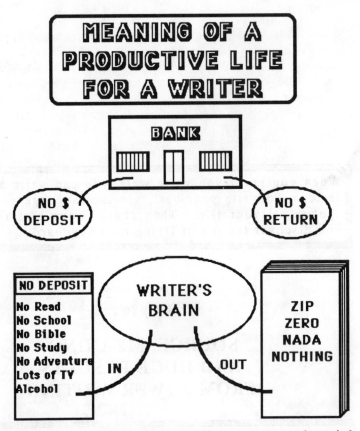

Still other books contain gold, but you need a pick and shovel to find it. It's as if a bank put a hold on the writer's deposits and then bounced checks. Readers have to dig real hard, to encounter some small treasures buried under several layers of self inflating language and complicated sentence construction. The writer had the treasure, but nobody could get to it.

You can fix overdraw; simply write truthfully within the confines of your knowledge and ability. Do some research and borrow from someone else's bank. Few book buyers read any book cover to cover anyway. So if you reveal only what you know truthfully, the exchange of their money for your knowledge or experience will be fair.

No matter how you go about it, fix under-deposited head knowledge before you write. Normally, it takes time to put enough deposits into your head so you can write. Many editors believe you need to be about 40 yrs old before you have something worthwhile to say. Read Proverbs I, and you will learn: "Wisdom calls aloud in the street, she raises her voice in the public squares." Take extra enrichment courses in school, study at home, travel, read, and talk to smart people.

Is your deposit on hold? Mark Twain said his writing was simple, like water. Other great literary geniuses wrote like wine. More people drink water. **Don't bury your riches!** Don't get illusions of literary grandeur. Just write the way you talk.

Look, you decided to take money for crafting words to teach, tell a story, gossip, or relate. If you write to impress your customers with your grandiloquence, then they won't enjoy what you wrote, but you get an ego blast from what you forced them to wade through. Therefore, YOU should pay THEM.

Today, we now have all kinds of tests to make sure we write for the audience available. Some computer programs kick out hard-to-comprehend words. In today's books, "big" is the right adjective for pictures, not words. I played tennis a few years back with a TV writer. When I asked him what kind of writing he did, he joked, "Mostly home, for money." You'll end up writing that way for real if you don't learn a lot before you write.

---

Here is a writing truth bureaucrats seldom learn:
**LENGTH WILL NEVER COVER UP
A LACK OF DEPTH.**

---

In 1961 I spent some time with John L Springer, who taught me the secret of writing success. He wrote profitably for the Associated Press, then more profitably as a freelancer. He now publishes the latest and greatest in business reports, tax tips, and money saving tricks. (TPR Publishing, 81 Montgomery St, Scarsdale, New York). In his advertising brochure, he explains that building wealth is not a function of making money, but in **keeping the money** you make. No other publication teaches you better. Beyond that, his work is a good study guide for any aspiring writer. It's crystal clear and concise. He specializes in delivering the most information in the fewest, easy-to-understand words.

This is what he taught me: "Publications compete with a variety of other media for the reader's time. If you can't send your message in a few words, the reader will abandon you."

Get your deposit off hold. Write with all the juice you have available. When you write, you need to be able to draw the last two cents worth out of your brain bank.

## DELIVER 100% OF THE POWER IN YOUR CREATIVE RESERVOIR!

As a writer, you need to work at staying in good physical, emotional, and mental shape. Otherwise, two sertious thoughts in a row might not produce much more than a headache.

Writing is a chore which inactivates everything but your mind. The mind functions best in a healthy body. Take care of your health. You may have noticed, you require regular maintenance. Eat right; exercise regularly. Buy a dog and walk it daily. Purchase a bicycle and ride at least three times a week. Play tennis. Swim. Do SOMETHING; your writing will reflect health. The best exercise for writers is aerobic exercise done at least three times a week. Also, choose an exercise which clears your mind. Weight lifting might not be the best; you need to do something which forces you to concentrate.

## WRITER'S ATMOSPHERE

### Effects on your battery

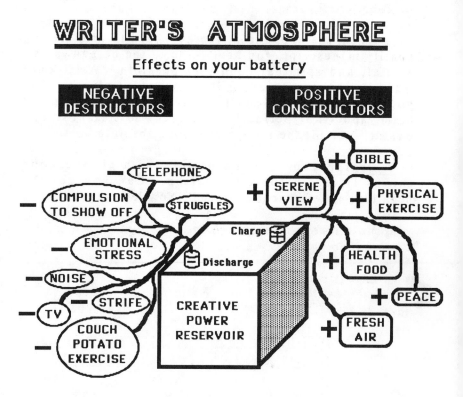

**NEGATIVE DESTRUCTORS**

**POSITIVE CONSTRUCTORS**

— TELEPHONE

— COMPULSION TO SHOW OFF

— STRUGGLES

— EMOTIONAL STRESS

— NOISE

— STRIFE

— TV

COUCH POTATO EXERCISE

Charge

Discharge

CREATIVE POWER RESERVOIR

+ SERENE VIEW

+ BIBLE

+ PHYSICAL EXERCISE

+ HEALTH FOOD

+ PEACE

+ FRESH AIR

Besides staying in top condition, keep negative drain out of our own life, and don't allow anyone else to drain your account. If you spend energy on someone else's problems, or let strife into your life, your account will be temporarily on hold. Thus, you won't be able to pour out the total wealth in your brain bank for your readers. Always un-list your phone number. Be careful giving it out. It jangles with a lot of un-necessary traffic. I tell people, "Oh, I'll have to call you; a lot of the time my computer is talking on the phone through a modem and can't be disturbed."

Sleep well. That's another reason to get plenty of exercise. Failure to get good sleep will cause you to arrive at the keyboard a bit groggy. Fatigue will show in your writing.

When you show up at the keyboard to produce top quality manuscript, you have to be in the best physical, mental, and spiritual condition possible. Write only when your batteries are fully charged. Only then can you focus clearly on master-crafting the paragraph at hand, and fit it perfectly into the whole manuscript. Result: you hit the reader with your absolute best.

Charge your writing battery with all the good things listed in the illustration. Can you get the negatives out of your life? Good! Now let's take off!

*Main text in New York 10 pt.*

# Chapter 10

## MAKE YOUR BOOK IRRESISTIBLE!
## MOLD YOUR CONTENTS

"I just have to buy this book," she screamed. Frantically, she fought off the store's threatening hordes for the last copy of my book. The police came and she ran from them. She knocked over bookcases, jumped partitions to get away, and finally paid cash. Then, I woke up. What was this dream about? The woman went crazy trying to buy one of my books. Why? She had just read my table of contents.

Naturally, you tell your readers what each chapter contains. But puff it up—-a lot. Next to the front and back covers, the table of contents is your best sales bait. If you're not enthusiastic about what you wrote, how can your readers be?

Your table of contents contains two parts: the chapter title, and the description. Before, during and after your book is completed, work and rework both parts. When the chapter titles really lure a reader, the chances of selling your book improve a lot. What would your prospective readers like to know most? What's the best you have to share? Once you answer those questions, try a more important one, "How can I describe my material in most glowing terms?"

Begin by calling up the Scratch Outline file, [D Scratch.otl RETURN]. On a MacIntosh, just double click your mouse on the Icon you labelled "Scratch." First, think about putting the chapters in a different order. Block and move all the chapters where you want them. In WordStar on an MS-Dos system, use ^KB at the beginning of the block and ^KK at the end, then move the cursor to a new location and hit ^KV. When your chapters are in most appealing order, kick off the insert mode (^V). Then just use the return key to go down through the chapter titles and type in the correct numbers; they'll erase the old ones and overwrite them.

On a MacIntosh, you can block easier because you merely depress the mouse button and drag the mouse through the information you want to move. Then save it

onto your clipboard {#X}.   It disappears from your
screen.   Move the cursor where you want the
information to re-appear; point and click on {#v paste}.

Keep polishing your chapter titles.   You need to
work these over three or four times before you allow
yourself the luxury of writing any sales copy underneath
them.   Always ask yourself, "Can I reword this to create a
better sales lure?"

The following list contains chapter headings for this
book.   We list the first idea, then the improved version.
You'll see final choices in this book's contents.

WHY YOU SHOULD WRITE QUICKLY.
JET-AGE SPEED WRITING,  MOST IMPORTANT
SPEED IS MORE IMPORTANT THAN OTHER  SKILLS

ORGANIZING YOUR IDEAS
 HELPING EVERYTHING TO FALL IN PLACE
THE KEY TO SPEED: ORGANIZING YOUR IDEAS

RESEARCH (Yuk!)
THE FUN OF MAKING DISCOVERIES
TAKE A BREAK; ENJOY THE JOY OF RESEARCH

WRITING THE PRODUCT
BLASTING OFF INTO YOUR MANUSCRIPT
HIT THE KEYBOARD PRODUCE HOT MANUSCRIPT

THINK THROUGH THE  PROJECT GRAPHICALLY
LETTING PICTURES HELP YOU TELL YOUR STORY
 LET PICTURES PRODUCE THOUSANDS OF EXTRA
WORDS .

REWRITING  (Ugh!)
WATCHING TIRED COPY COME ALIVE
WEEDING YOUR WORD GARDEN

Once the chapter titles have been carefully and thoughtfully reworded, concentrate on the chapter descriptions. Your table of contents is the best place for any humor you've found. Try your hardest to include some one-liners near the first chapter. If you succeed, you send the reader a message: "This book will be fun to read." In *EVERYBODY'S KNIFE BIBLE*, we admonished that a dull blade is more dangerous than a sharp one. In the Table of Contents, you'll read, "Too lazy to sharpen yours? **Suture self.**"

Convert your ideas so they are clearly reader benefits. Tell your readers how your ideas will work wonders **for them.** Don't tell readers they will learn; tell them you will teach. Learning is a chore. When you teach, they can sit back and soak it in. Rather than tell them they're going to learn how to become a better person, let your buyers know that with this book, **they will become better persons!** *EVERYBODY'S KNIFE BIBLE* advances outdoorsmen into the 21st Century; it doesn't mention trigonometry, memory or practical work.

Of course, when you think the table of contents is complete, let it sit for awhile in storage, then pull it up a few days later. Then start all over again. Your table of contents deserves as much rewriting as a presidential inauguration speech.

Once you have it done, you can relax and be confident. Anyone who picks up your book and finds out what's inside will buy it.

*Text done in Helvetica 12 pt.*

Not only do you want to write quickly. You want your readers to grasp your message quickly. To accomplish that, you have to play pretty word music for their concentration levels. It's like a concert--drums, lights up, tune, crescendo, drop to faint melody---then back up. One great instrument any writer can learn to play at a writing concert is humor. It provides the readers' minds with notes of relief so they relax, then get the full impact of your composition easily and in record time.

## Chapter 11

### ENTERTAINMENT TONIGHT
### MAKING YOUR READERS LAUGH OUT LOUD

"All my friends are compulsive bargain hunters; they only like me because I am 50% off."

With only a decent bit of humor, you'll develop a special, highly appreciative audience. Right now, the back cover for my book, *Speed Spanish for Gringos* reads, "This book contains the **welfare mentality method** for getting a vocabulary: **Don't work for it; steal it!**

Does humor sell? You bet! In 1988, <u>The American Survival Guide Magazine</u> reviewed <u>*Everybody's Knife Bible*</u> and said it was funny. The word "funny" always means extra sales.

Your readers may never know why, but they'll remember your instruction a lot better because you made them laugh. Laughing is the best way for a reader to take a break. She leaves you. She may drop your book in her lap and giggle. Then, when she comes back from the vacation you just gave her, her mind will be fresh and receptive.

TV sitcoms should tell you: comedy pays. In books, though, it does far more than entertain. If you write for a special interest group, (such as outdoorsmen), you can wrap the whole book in a tone of derisive humor, pander to a rebellious spirit, and create a sitcom full of the best outdoor how-to information in the world. That's what we do in the Green Beret Outdoor Survival Guides. Even though the books are about a live-or-die serious topic, I think in funny terms often, and flaunt it. When you do the same, writing is fun, and your readers get your message best.

I've performed at comedy stores in California, Virgina, and Nevada. I enjoy a good joke. Stand up comedy is a difficult art form, however, because the performer must first learn to deal with a tremendous fear—-fear of failure---no laughs. Also, timing is critical. Then too, some drunk heckles you, and you have to handle. Thinking on your feet under pressure can be tough.

Written humor is much easier. You can write a lot of it by formula. It works best on the reader, however, if it fits. Off subject jokes don't work well because they become interruptions, and annoy rather than amuse. Fit means: "will be funny to your (particular) reading audience," and, "is appropriate for the subject matter at hand."

How do you aim at an audience? Listen to the words of Babaloo Mandell and Lowell Ganz, two of Hollywood's top writers, in a recent movie, City Slickers. The cowboy cook prays over the buried body of Jack Palance, the toughest cowboy ever. "Dear Lord, we give you Curly. Try not to piss him off."

Are you writing to a group of married females? Try it this way:

"Dear Lord, I give you my husband. Don't you dare mess with his motorcycle"

Is you audience mostly a male one? Then try it this way at your wife's funeral:

"Dear Lord, I give you my wife. Don't even think of taking away her credit cards," or, "Try not to leave a mess in her kitchen." If you're cruel, "I hope now she's moving up to heaven, cause for forty years down here, I watched her go the other way."

The second part of "fit" deals with "appropriate for your subject matter." Believe it or not, how tightly you stick to this rule depends on the software you use to produce camera ready copy. If all you can do with your writing equipment is create pages full of words, make sure your humor fits. Also, segue into it smoothly.

On the other hand, a camera ready text-flow software gives you more latitude because you can use side-bars and call-out boxes. The boxes give the reader a warning that this material may not fit, so you don't jar the reader. In addition, the extraneous material in the boxes doesn't have to be absorbed during any particular thought transfer; the reader gets to pick it up when she wants it. Therefore, you don't have to segue smoothly or stay right on subject.

Speaking of "on-subject," let's talk about off-color; don't. It's not creative to punch in four letter words, and it violates the law of the first Book ever and all-time best seller, The Bible. It also offends lots of people who understand words containing more than one syllable. Eddie Murphy's comedy full of four letter words isn't very creative... But he performs at his audience's level of comprehension. It gets laughs because he panders to those who revel in the camaraderie one gets from laughing peers, most of whom conduct their lives on the same moral plane. If you don't believe camaraderie helps create laughter, ask yourself, why do TV sitcoms employ laugh tracks all the time?

Writing clean comedy is easy. Work it in so that your writing doesn't collapse if your joke misses. You want it to read like part of the book, and tickle your reader—sort of by accident. You'll give the reader the same funny jolt we all get when humor is truly extemporaneous. Go ahead, reach for it; your test readers will tell you if the joke doesn't fit. That's why you employ them.

In the old days, we had to rely on our own memories to properly use a gag file. In his book, How to be Funny, Steve Allen writes, "Read funny books." That's fine, but how do you remember jokes to use at the proper time? What is this thing called a "good sense of comedic timing?" For writers, timing comedy is like an open book during a high school exam. You simply take the joke out of your memory or files and plug it into the place in your manuscript where it fits the subject.

Spend a couple hundred dollars on humor books. Almost all of those books list jokes by subject. As soon as you have a good joke, choose from four methods of presentation:

        A. Use a side-bar.
        B. Use a call-out box.
        C. Work it into the text.
        D. Use a cartoon.

Both A and B only require that the joke match-up be close to your subject. Of course, cartoons must be on subject, need not flow into text, but stand on their own to provide relaxed examination and eye relief.

Where can you get material? I listen to radio comedy hours, TV standups such as Carson and Leno, etc. If the show is live and I have a computer nearby, I type the material into the data base as fast as I hear it.

3 5 x 10

Remember diagraming sentences in school? Comedy diagrams the same way. The main subject can have several sub-subjects which might substitute for it. Like pronouns, they take the place of the main subject and merely allow the joke to fit in with other material. The premise or situation takes your readers into a make believe place where they vicariously feel or experience the interaction. The setup leads the reader to believe you will go in a certain direction, so much so that his mind advances to that logical conclusion. The punch line yanks him back away from the direction of the setup and surprises him. Thus the laughter.

Keep in mind when recording that you don't have to get the premise or setup right. Punch line and Subject are enough. Later, you can go back into your DataBase and remodel the joke with a new premise and setup.

Once you've collected a good number of jokes, it's time to index them. Keep track of your jokes by subject, punch line, premise or setup on just about any data base software.

If you want to work with your gag files on paper, you can print out, then separate the sheets. Use a three hole punch on them, and add index tabs by subject and punch line so your files are easy to work with. Equally as good, merely call up the subject heading you want on the computer screen, and re-work the premise and set-up so it fits into your manuscript.

Try this joke. A dying man wants to take his money with him. He gives a million in cash each to a priest, a minister, and a rabbi, all with the understanding that they'll put the money in the casket with him after he's dead. They agree. But the Catholic priest took a little out for church repairs, and the Protestant bought new hymnals. Later, feeling guilty, the two got together and confessed their sins to one another, "Maybe we shouldn't feel so bad," said the minister, "let's go talk to the Rabbi." When the Rabbi heard what they had done, he became angry with them. "How could you, men of the cloth, take a dead man's money! For shame! But I, belonging to the ancient holy faith of the one true God, kept honor to his trust in a spirit of holiness and honesty. I put ALL of the money in my bank, and gently laid in his casket, a check for the full amount."

Put that joke in your data base this way. Subject: Tightwads, money or religions. Punch line: I put the cash in my bank, and wrote him a check for the whole amount. Setup: self righteous rabbi castigates other preachers for taking money not belonging to them. Premise: Three pastors entrusted with money by a dying man. Two spend a little of the money. The third rebukes and condemns them---but then proves to have stolen the whole amount.

Here's the same joke again—-modified for a Catholic audience in Ireland: A dying millionaire who belonged to neither faith called in a priest and a Scottish preacher to his deathbed. He asked both to honor him with his last dying wish—-to help him take his money with him. They promised faithfully to put the money in his casket. Leaving him, they took a million each. But the Catholic took some of the money out to buy altar wine. To get his conscience cleared he went to the preacher and confessed. "How could you?" cried the Scottsman. "I kept the faith; I did what was right. I deposited the money into our convalescent hospital's life insurance plan, and bought him a lifetime annuity."

> Incidentally, most writers suplement their income with a side business. I'm going to open a bar soon in Palm Beach Florida. I'll name it, "THE SENATOR KENNEDY BAR." I'll make millions! (24 drink minimum.)

Most good comedians deliver; someone else writes. You do both. Take a good joke, custom tailor it for your use, and deliver it with care. Custom tailor means you write the joke in a way that your audience can accept. You say derisive humor, jabbed at the KKK, won't work in the Alabama news? Try any magazine written for a black readership.

See, almost everybody laughs at a joke when it's aimed at their pet peeve or enemy. That's why Carson did so well when he said "it was so cold——they discovered an attorney with his hands in his **own** pockets."

Where else can you get material? Several good joke brokers make a living selling funny material. If you do a lot of public speaking, and most authors do, you can use Robert Orben. He publishes jokes monthly for $72 a year. I talked to him, however, and he was mighty adamant about his material **not** appearing in print when he said, "a major publisher just shredded thousands of books due to a court order." If you copy his material straight into your book, your readers may try you, but so will his attorneys—in a lawsuit.

It's not that hard to roll your own——jokes. Read a few books on how to write comedy such as *Comedy Writing Secrets* by Melvin Hellitzer. Also, try *How to Write and Sell Your Sense of Humor* by Gene Perret. I like Steve Allen, who to me exhibits the highest intellectual skill in analyzing humor. Read his book, *How to be Funny*. This is perhaps the best because Steve's wit is just about as sharp as his intellect. One other factor in going with Steve—-you can buy the book in trade paper for under $8.

One good method of setting up an audience is to make them expect one thing, and then deliver another. (I used that technique in developing a relationship with a wife once. Caused a divorce).

Jonathan Winters is quoted, during a serious interview about his career: "I couldn't wait for success, so I went ahead without it."

Can you use that? How would it fit into this book? First, write the joke on your screen, then block it [^KB ^KK] and write it to disc [^KW]. Name it, JOKE.INS (insert) and figure out later where it should go.

How about Chapter 1 on the importance of speed: "When you're so broke, and so down, that you can't wait for success, go ahead and write without it." How about Chapter 8 on time/write planning? You have everything organized: subject, outline, photos, and you can't wait for success. Well, start writing without it. . .

Use each joke only once in your book. The second time isn't funny. Humor is best when it's true, and you lie to your reader if you try to get away with a re-run.

With humor, you can electrify your readers, and supply the literary world with RIGOR. Of course, you should always respect the more serious writers, because they supply MORTIS.

*Times, 12 pt.*

> Quick **commuter travel** occurs on a jet airplane. If a writer wants to get to the end of a manuscript fast, he needs to book **computer travel**. No jet flies without fuel, and no computer flies without software. There's stuff out there today that will make your computer fly like never before.

## Chapter 12

## WORKING WONDERS WITH SOFTWARE

Letting computer software work for you is about the same as enjoying maid service in a hotel. Instead of scouring your bathroom, tossing out your trash and checking your sheets, computer maids correct your grammar, toss out your mistakes, and correct your spelling. Your writing life flows easier because the menial chores are done by the a computer servant--and, you don't even have to tip.

Both IBM's and the MacIntosh offer maid service. What the Mac will do easier for more bucks is import graphics. That's like room service. Macs are also getting cheaper, and they feature graphics environment management, which means you can point and click on the computer screen to make it do its magic rather than remembering keyboard commands.

Buy a magazine for your computer. Read the ads. Order a catalog featuring software and other items. *Home Office Computing Magazine* offers the latest and greatest developments in our field. One such recent hot tip: Buy an old XT personal computer. Then remove the 8088 Microprocessor out and replace it with a new with an Intel 8088-2 for under $15 to make it fly with the big boys.

For Mac owners, the magazines are indispensable. Here are a few examples of Mac software. MicroSoft Word 4.0. Cost $245. It's probably the work horse on the Mac for writers. It features a spell checker, automatic indexing , mail merging, an integrated outliner. I've been working with mine for a year, and I probably use 20% of its power. The same company produces MicroSoft Write for $85, which contains double the 20% I use of their Word.

MacWrite II, 1.1. This is the offshoot of the original, which set the standard for Mac's way back when a 512K RAM was a big deal. (We now enjoy brain sizes past 4 meg.) Cost: $139.

WordPerfect 2.0. Cost $279. This one has an enhanced graphics capability. Therefore, you don't have to kick out of the program to insert a graphic, and if you move the graphic, the text will reflow for you.

Write Now 2.2 with Grammatik Mac included. Cost $119. Huge spelling dictionary of 135,000 words. Grammatik Mac is worth $59, and I wouldn't write without it. That means this power house program is yours for $60. That's a steal.

MacProof 3.2.1 cost $115. This examines your writing and proof reads for you without your having to exit your word processor. It checks you word usage, punctuation, style, and structure, as well as spelling and capitalization.

GRAPHICS. SuperPaint 2.0. This is the program I use. It converts from draw to paint on one click. It also imports into most page maker programs. The new upgrade does amazing color work, but we print black and white books. Aldus graphic software packages produce Postscript, so you get smoother lines on your print out.

Even if you happen to be the winner of the national spelling bee, have the maid correct your spelling. It's best to wait until the third or fourth rough draft before hitting your script with your spell checker.

I was married and sinking when I began to write this book. My exasperated wife commanded me not to write another #$%& book!. After she went to sleep at 11:30 PM, I would drop out of bed and crawl on all fours into another room to work. Most of this book was born between midnight and zero-dark-thirty.

To say the least, the manuscript was sloppier than a bachelor's motor home. So, I paid $20 to a third grade school teacher to read it over and make corrections. She was tough, and I got back notes like, "dummy!" I put her corrections into the computer, reprinted, and paid another $20 to a friend's wife who had a masters in English. More corrections. Then I paid $450 to a manuscript consultant in West Los Angeles. I got back enough red color on my manuscript to make a bull charge. Now, once I'd incorporated all these changes into the manuscript, wouldn't you think I had scrubbed it clean enough?

Enter two manuscript scrubbers, both of whom are quicker than all the humans you can hire. Grammatic III cost $99 and RightWriter costs $95. Don't print out without them. Both of these take some time on the computer to use because they are so thorough. Why? The programs assume you are a lower level writer, so they do things like tag sentence fragments and tell you to use a verb. But the good stuff it catches gives you confidence that you have scrubbed your writing as clean as a Hilton hotel room. Just consider my own case. After all the corrections given me by test readers and editors, Grammatic III found two instances of double words, three places where I had opened quotations and failed to close them," and several sentences too long for the average reader to comprehend (more than 30 words long, like this one). RightWriter did about the same, but the software company reports that their new versions are quicker, bigger (75,000 word dictionaries) and scrutinize your manuscript more closely. You can be the judge. Still, if you were to buy them both, you would only spend half what I did to pay editors, and the software **never misses.** Grammatic kicks out high level words. RightWriter shows you a list of those words and it shows others which induce a negative effects on readers.

When Grammatik finished this book, it reported: Average word syllable count between 1.42 and 1.58. Grade level reading difficulty between 6th and 8th. It also summarized the numbers of short sentences (under 14 words) as well as the long ones). Of course, to determine the ease of readability requires comparison. So, in order to find out how you really write, you can ask Grammatik to compare your writing to: A life insurance policy, the Gettysburg Address, and Hemingways short stories. The comparisons come up on the screen in a bar graph so you can see immediately how readable your book will be. This book beat the first two, but placed just behind Hemingway.

RightSoft produces Rightwriter obtainable by writing to 4545 Samuel St, Sarasota, Florida, 34233 (Phone 813-923-0233) This is a typical report: I used 48 uncommon words. (which make the manuscript difficult to read.) It saddens me to learn that Gettysburg (my computer tossed it out) is no longer a common word to our language.

RightWriter now gives me a Strength Index of 0.65 (good, but could be improved). My Descriptive Index is 0.62, and the comment is: "The use of adjectives and adverbs is within normal range." Furthermore, it tells me my Readability Index is 6.71, which means a seventh grader can read this chapter, with the exception of uncommon words.

If you use WordPerfect, you can macro to get direct access to the software and thus let it help you scrub your manuscript while you write.

Both of these programs deserve your attention. My pastor uses RightWriter to kick out words too complex for many in his congregation to understand. Both programs pay for themselves the first time you employ them. More importantly, however, they set a standard to which most competitive writers now rise. That means: No matter how diligently you try and clean up your manuscripts by yourself, you'll probably be recognized as substandard if you don't employ one or both of these software packages.

Use these programs and you can probably write sloppy text in the dark. My own laptop has a backlit screen so I can check my writing if I want to, but I write a lot with my eyes closed. I don't pay much attention to spelling because I know my checkers will catch almost everything when I'm finished. My eyes will probably thank me when I turn 60. Also, my brain thanks me now. I have less to worry about.

More important, though, is this: I am free from worry. The spelling, grammar, diction and syntax will be maid-serviced electronically, so I only have one place to apply all of my brain. All I need do is write what I think about, and my thinking won't be confined by menial details.

Fiction writers need only think ahead to the twists in the plot, the dialogue, and the character development. They can actually enjoy the story as they jot down the bare essentials. Non- fiction writers can concentrate on syntax, chronology or humor. In addition to the above, however, there is a new art form emerging for print media producers which requires constant concentration.

For a quite a while, we've know you can dress too busy. It means, too much going on, too much color, too much contrast, and, perhaps, too many accessories. Likewise, you can dress a page "too busy," and affront the reader. But the page creating art form goes much further. Today, most of your reading audience copes daily with information anxiety.

Students graduating from school are less educated than ever before, but the world they face is more complex and demands more technological know-how. The distance between what they know and what they need to know when they graduate is bigger. So is the anxiety it causes.

The anxiety caused by that invades every facet of our lives. Almost every American faces a great fear when trying to learn and speak a foreign language. Mental blocks on arithmetic are common. High school seniors fear and can't pass a final, high school graduation exam. Recently, fourteen percent of high school graduates couldn't locate the USA on a world map. International test results place over a dozen foreign country students ahead of U.S. students in science and math.

What does this mean to a writer? It means, more than ever before, you have to beg (on your knees) for the readers' attention. Consider America's great love affair with TV. Today, we acquire knowledge and information much the same way cave men communicated—-through pictures. Of course, video media is easier on the eyes and more fun to watch. Audio-visual producers are willing to spoon feed and pander to their audiences. What can you do?

Not only must you write simple prose; you must draw pictures and use photos extensively. Not only do you have to draw pictures; you have to label them with short words. Finally, you have to learn to use type styling, word emphasis and white space so that each page presents the reader with an easy molehill rather than a tough mountain (of words).

But you're a writer; you write print media and compete for the reader's attention. How can you compete? What's new is to lay out your pages with pictures charts and graphs so you lure the reader. Quark and TypeStyler let you design a page which will hand feed information into your readers brain. Page layout is the new writer's science.

Basically, you design a page according to subject. If your material is dry, you need to lure your readers and dazzle them. Advertising copy and cover material require that kind of pizazz. On the other hand, if you are writing stuff you know the reader will sit on the edge of his chair and beg for, regular print without clever use of white space will do. Just make sure to choose a nice sans seriff font and an easy size, like 12 pt, to read. If you write to a young audience, you can get away with a lesser size print. If, however, your primary reading audience is over 50, use a bold print style and go as big as 14 points with your type size. Remember, you're going to adjust the whole thing so it fits 32 page signatures when you finish writing anyway. If you can't adjust by adding script or illustrations, you may have to adjust with a font size change.

Look at the way we did things with *Hammock*. For almost every way to use a hammock, I drew some kind of illustration. I then labelled them so I could identify them later and integrate them into Quark by importing them from SuperPaint 2.0. I shrunk down the illustrations which had no fine detail or writing on them. When they looked OK in the check print, I shipped them.

You can learn to be clever at page layout. However, you can't do it by hand unless you live south of the border and your Spanish name is Manual Labor. Modern day page makers are the only way to go. Three of the most popular are: Ventura Publisher, PageMaker, and QuarkXpress. I hired a consultant in Hawaii, Mac Publishing (1-808-848-2824), who advised me to go with Quark on a MacIntosh. The learning curve is steep, as is the cost, (over $500) but the results are superb, and I am still learning. Even with that cost, Quark wants another $225 per year to offer you help over the telephone. Pagemaker reports their technical advice is free.

If you stay with an IBM system, several programs will do maid service you can only dream about. One of those maid service chores is <u>file management</u>. Begin with the best: Q-DOS-II. Gazelle Systems, 42 N. University Ave, Suite 10, Provo, Utah 84601 produces a file maintenance software program that will pay for itself in the first month. Call them at 801-377-1288, and they'll send you free literature.

They call this program, "The amazingly fast hard-disk file manager." But, it does its magic with computers operating on two floppies (my laptop) as well.

How could anybody want to spend time learning MS-DOS when they could use Q-Dos? The program displays all your files, along with a menu to do any task. You merely move the cursor to choose any operation and hit return.

Not only is the learning curve miles shorter, but the program performs a lot faster than a word processor. I save about a half hour a day cleaning up my files. Q-Dos allows you to tag files selectively, push a few keys and watch them move, rename, or erase from your screen.

Any writer absolutely needs to to save her work everyday on a master disk (either B or A drive floppy). That way, one special place has the latest update on your manuscript. Thus you can scrub your writing clean on your regular work disc.

Q-DOS ("Q" for Quick) solves the "make a backup copy" problem in a jiffy. Your latest and greatest just replaced yesterday's product. As soon as you record all that on your disc, label it with a pen. Pull the disk out of the drive and record the date of revision along with the title of your work and any other material on the disc.

The result: Every time you quit, the most up-to-date revisions are stored safely, and you are free to travel with your working manuscript disc. Fear of loss no longer exists, and you can find your most recent upgrade easily.

As you near the completion of any book, you will add or subtract pages from various chapters in order to finish with full signatures. If you convert from MS-Dos onto a Mac, you can adjust the print style and size so you fill printer signatures exactly. To get an even numbers of pages for every chapter, do this: On a Mac, you simply determine whether you need more or less body in your manuscript. For less, size down the illustrations {Apple M}. For more, add illustrations, photos, or text. Text comes in one of three flavors, regular print, call-out boxes or side-bars. By using one of the latter two, you can write something which does NOT need to flow in with your regular writing, such as a quote or one-liner joke.

### COMMUNICATING WITH OTHER COMPUTERS

When we discussed research, we mentioned a modem (short computer word for modulator, demodulator.) My own NEC laptop contains a 2400 Baud modem. Tele-communications software makes it do magic.

One such program is Telix, a shareware offered through most of the BBS's (Bulletin Board Systems) all over the world. You merely download the program, which comes complete with extensive documents, and try it out. If you like it, you register on your honor by sending $35 to the copyright holders. DAK mail order includes Procomm with most lap tops.

Of course, other options are available. Choose your telecommunications software with a Z- Modem protocol if you can. X-Modem was the first out and is still employed by a lot of old users, but the newer Z is faster.

Now, you have the software capability to produce great manuscripts in record time. You can save each day's work with precision and safety, and you have access to research, BBS's and other writers through your Modem and its supporting software. What's left?

## USING COMPUTERS FOR OTHER PURPOSES

As soon as sales begin to multiply and the money rolls in, you have problems: How can you manage to remember all of your customers? Should you print more books? What kinds of things happen to profit if you implement a new idea? Can you project your earnings for the year after next?

All the above questions and many more are answered with a couple of computer software packages. Basically, you'll need a spread sheet to help budget for future expansion and help prepare your financial statements and taxes. You also need to manage your customer lists. In addition, it will help if you can keep your checkbook straight.

Hiring office staff creates problems of its

own. The current trend of thought in America pits employee against management. The new morality gives little credence to company loyalty or honesty. Workers compensation invites fraud, and frail humans either don't show up, take an extra day off, or "borrow" the company's proceeds. Also, some states, (notably Hawaii) make it more than burdensome if you hire anybody. By the time you fill out all the forms, answer the phone calls from bureaucrats and deal with audits, you could write an extra book or two.

As book sales soar, you may expand and think about hiring people. Think first about buying a new machine. If you like management problems, additional business interference with self-inflated bureaucrats, and more paper work, hire people and pay them a salary, especially in the U.S. On the other hand, buy a new computer and printer, and you'll have a full time worker who never calls in late or goes on strike or steals from you. Use your computer(s). You can buy an additional computer for $600 and dedicate it to one or two non-writing tasks.

In a modern, high production publishing company, you need at least two computers. You need to produce manuscript, graphics, ad copy, letters and special mail-out pieces. You need to do bookkeeping, tax reporting and database management. Why? Consider what a modern, self-publishing writer does. The job of authorship goes far beyond the mere transfer of though through printed word.

Authors today write advertising copy and promotional stuff on a Pagemaker type program. From a second machine they generate graphics copy, newsletters, and excerpts (portions of their best writing) to promote books or newsletters.

They roll over to other stations and input data for a mailing list. From that list, the author will generate mailing labels so several editors and reviewers receive his message. The computer dials individual names on the list automatically. Headsets save the trouble of holding a telephone ear piece, so both hands are free to type orders.

Perhaps a telecommunications program occupies another, through which the writer does his research or transfers files to and from the home office. In addition, the modem sends and receives electronic mail through a regular service.

One other program for high-volume publishers is Quicken, which allows the computer owner to write all his checks in a jiffy. At the same time, the program keeps a running bank balance. Repeat checks, such as mortgage or car payments are made automatically—-same payee, same amount. The checks come with tractor feeds for any printer, so you can spend money faster than Zsa Zsa Gabor.

Of course, you can do all of the above functions on a MacIntosh. Program writers for the Mac have duplicated and tried to improve upon every program available for IBM clones. Two differences set Mac software aside. One, Mac programs are user friendly because they employ a point and click method of operation with your mouse. Just click on what you want off a pull down menu and the computer does the work. Two, the programs cost more.

Computer software follows the second law of economics: "If you got the money, you can save and use the time. Saving and using time is probably how you got money in the first place."

Software is what makes that difference, and the newer machines with the larger computer brains (RAM) handle some powerful software. Once you own the tools, however, you can rapid-write for the rest of your life as an author, and enjoy the income for a long time.

*Geneva 12 pt.*

> To buy quick production tools, you'll need money.
> Here's how to get your books to produce enough.

> Do you think a writer merely produces manuscript and then rakes in the cash? You're wrong. Never expect your book to sell through wholesalers or bookstore chains automatically so you can retire. It simply won't occur. Whether you write for another publisher or self publish, you just have to participate in sales. That's the bad news. But, the good news is: **it's easy.**

## Chapter 13

### KEEP THY SELF GREEN
### HELP THY BOOK HARVEST CASH

If you want to be rich and famous, discover an audience you can write for. Then cause that audience to discover you. Once you accomplish this feat, just keep turning the crank.

Successful singers keep turning the crank. Somebody estimated that Tony Bennet sang "I Lost My Heart in San Francisco" over 10,000 times. Remember Sammy Davis, Jr? I'll bet he sang "Mr Bo Jangles" enough to do it without cue cards.

See, ALL commercially successful writing needs one vital factor to succeed: a targeted audience. Most rejection slips from publishers go to those writers who write well enough, but mis-target their work product. That's why you see this message over and over again from editors: "Read our magazine before submitting." Here at Path Finder, we receive query letters on literary product we are not set up to sell. It's decent product, and we can see how to locate and make sales to the audience, but we would have to hire and/or re-organize in order to bring it all together. We pass.

Would you like to sell your book in huge quantities? Write product to please your targeted audience. Then conduct an aggressive sales campaign. Sales are important because you learn during sales how to better target the audience to whom you sell.

From the beginning, Path Finder's book sales were impressive. But, our sales efforts were weak. I had no idea how sales happen, or how the market place works. "Margin-of-profit" was a foreign term to me, and I didn't know who paid for freight, insures packages, or what "30 Days Net" signified. Even though we did all right, sales were nowhere near what they could have been.

I didn't know the market. I mused, "If a magazine says The Green Beret Books are great, everyone should want one." That was a rather short-sighted thought.

Investigate your market before you write. I wrote *Everybody's Knife Bible* primarily to boost sales of my other books. I figured, "Not everybody is a survivalist, but **everybody** uses a knife, and I knew a lot of ways to use a knife in the woods. Of course, the book was Boy Scout clean. I stayed away from anything rough and tumble.

So—with confidence, I talked to the book buyer for Big-5 Sporting Goods in L.A. I pitched him my Knife Bible. "Sure," he said, "send me a copy. If we like it, our first order will be for 600 copies; just give me a price." I hung up the phone, and jumped for joy. This was it, the big one! Even if we make only $2 per book net, the profit is $1200, and they'll reorder forever.

Like a hungry cat waiting for a fat mouse, I waited a couple weeks after sending the book and the quote. Then, I called to close the sale.

"**No way!**" he said. "That book violates our corporate image." Then he went on to tell me why. He said, "The cover is offensive; the tone of the book is just too rough."

I was broken. After I thought it over for a while, however, I had to praise God for this new opportunity He had given me to improve my product.

I wrote the buyer, thanking him for the opportunity to present my product to Big 5. I also asked for an opportunity to call and ask what parts of the book I could remove to make it a book they would buy.

Then I wrote our cover designer, Phyllis Hughes, at 250 Acton Street, Carlisle, Mass 01741, and asked for a change. Clever her—-she designed a cover with the same colors, but merely converted them to trees and green. That way, old customers recognize the book as ours, and we still satisfy the book buyers who don't want to play Rambo.

Here's the moral of the story: You can't write and sell well for a market you haven't investigated. Granted, your book will often be brand new, full of controversial ideas and novel ways of doing things, so a sales test is difficult. What do you do? Run a small number of copies, (say about 100) and send them to important people connected with your topic. You kick out camera ready copy off your computer set up, collate in your photos and illustrations, then use a copy machine. Spiral binding works best for us, because the illustrations we use require that our book lies flat when open. Remember, you write on a computer, so a text change can happen in a New York minute.

You want your book to sell, so you concentrate on production quality—sales quality. In order of importance, it goes: The lure of the cover, the hook in the title and sub-title, the line of sales zingers on the back cover, the bait in the table of contents, the shine in the illustrations, and finally, the weight in your writing, **in that order**.

As you know, most book buyers don't completely read the books they buy. So sales don't have much to do with syntax. Book sales are made for the same reason car sales are made—it's the polish. Format your book to sell. Remember, they buy before they read.

When we tell you to write a book in 53 days, we are telling you to write a 128 page book, sized 5-1/2 X 8-1/2 inches. You may plan to write a much longer book. Don't. As a matter of fact, if you think your book will run more than 256 pages, cut the manuscript in half. Long manuscripts produce better income if they are split into two separate books. Publish the first. If it sells well, the sequel will follow successfully.

You'll discover another reason for doing this when you order both our *Green Beret Outdoor Guides*. Those two could have combined to make one big book. The way it is, we get two sales for $12.95 each. One big book for $25.95 would be a tough sale. Especially to our market. Worse, you are asking one buyer to buy material she may not need. In this book for example, experienced writers would much rather pay half for the information in book two. When I had twenty chapters written, I graded them with A's and B's according to how appealing I thought they might be. Half the A's and half the B's made a complete book.

Experts in direct sales have known for years that sales are lost for one of five reasons. Lack of knowledge: (the buyer doesn't understand the pitch or didn't hear ALL the product benefits. Lack of money: price too high, competition has cheaper product. Lack of interest: your product is well put together, but who cares? Lack of trust: Sales guy is too slick and unbelievable. Finally, no exigency in the sale: it's a great deal, but you can get it anytime; if you wait, it might go on sale.

You have to develop sales quality which conquers all of the above reasons why people don't buy things. As applied to book sales, you overcome the following:

Lack of knowledge: Make sure the pitch on your book is simple and direct. If the customer doesn't understand it, she won't buy it. Kill lack of knowledge. Make your sales pitch with fifth grade clarity. **Never** use a big word or a long sentence when fishing for customers.

Lack of money. You want to price your book to make a good profit, but you can't go crazy. Also, watch your competition. If someone releases a similar product which is cheaper than yours, your sales will drop severely. Overcome budget restrictions. Build product with an affordable price.

Lack of interest. You discover something new about a famous celebrity (JFK) who passed away, but who cares now? Don't write on an untimely subject. One big reason for speed writing is this: You go through the computer to print out and publish before anyone else can even get a start. Publishing is a highly competitive fight. As in war, you win when you get there first with the most.

Lack of trust. Stretch the truth just once in a book you write and the whole sales pitch goes belly-up. Engineer faith and trust. Make sure of your facts, and quote reviewers carefully when they praise your work.

Procrastination. Your product will sell a lot less if it features information the buyer doesn't really need NOW. Of all the things you can do with your back cover, the most important is to create a sense of urgency. Don't allow a buyer think it over. You want a sale now; not later.

Spend $9.95 at Para Publishing, Box 4232-496, Santa Barbara, CA 93140-4232, to purchase *Words That Sell*. Words such as "newest, latest," tell a reader he should buy now because everything else is old hat. You tell them, "You gotta have it, and you gotta have it now."

That's the reason Path Finder books go to other

markets. We sell in gun stores, surplus stores, military shops, and in most military outdoor mail order catalogs. People who need information about activities or hobbies in which they are involved don't want to wait for the information; they want it now.

The element of **now** also is a part of subject choice. Write something to a particular group whose hobby revolves around related products (such as sporting goods). If you do, you'll sell volumes even if your book doesn't gain popular acceptance. Why? Because your book can help manufacturers market their products.

Poynter calls marketing through other businesses the premium sales concept. Suppose you write a pleasant book about the history of your area, with nice lithography. Even before you go into production, try local banks on using your book as a premium gift to new customers. Go ahead and let the bank rewrite portions of your book so it includes the history of the bank, and therefore draws potential customers.

Direct mail advertising did a great job for us. However, if you plan to use direct mail flyers, go cheaply by co-op mailing them. Find another direct mail outfit which targets the same reading audience you do. Ask them to include your ads in the same envelope. We recently mailed to 2700 libraries for under two cents each. The price was cheap; the idea was dumb. In our case, we hadn't yet submitted our books for review to any of the journals regularly providing news to libraries. Few librarians will order anything blind, so we wasted our money. But the mail-out was cheap because we car-pooled it.

While direct mail doesn't do much, direct contact does. Use your phone. It costs 50-75 cents a piece to mail out literature and you get less respect than Rodney Dangerfield. On the other hand, phones provide you with a personal touch and insure that whatever you send will land right on target. Also—-you'll see a lot more of this in the future—-FAX your customers. Even if you don't have a FAX you can subscribe to MCI mail (800)-444-6245 and get 40 E-mail or FAX messages for only $10 per month. Only .25 cents for overnight. As mail gets worse and the price increases, E-mail will be the wave of the future.

Let's assume you have no idea how or where to sell your book. Can you maintain the absolutely necessary hot mental attitude it takes to make sales? Help yourself to become positive about your book. Like nobody else, you can learn what makes your book best. Talk to editors, send the product and your review material, and then call them back. You have to do both.

Recently we decided to release copyrights on the *Green Beret's Compass Course* to Army and Marine Generals. When I talked to the editor of Soldier of Fortune Magazine and told him I had sent copy to Col Robert Brown, the publisher, he said, "That's the black hole." Don't just send it. Call and make sure it landed.

But suppose your topic is really a rare one. Where in the heck are you going to find a reading audience? The most obvious thing to do is call a mailing list broker. You can order the lists in several ways. Index cards (to keep a record of calls and orders), regular size paper, or on computer diskette to print out from DBase software. For example, American Business Lists (402-331-7169) sent me a free catalog featuring lists of 14,000,000 businesses.

We ordered the list for fishing, camping, hiking and gun stores to sell our outdoor books. The company (ABL) will screen the list for duplicates, and are only too happy to furnish you with businesses which pay for a certain size display ad in their local yellow pages. That saves money and time; you sell the big stores first and easiest. In our case, we ordered the list for gun stores, but avoided mom 'n pop operations by taking display ads only. Also, we ordered the gun store list from 11 Western States so we could call from the East after hours. Later, we plan to call the Eastern States early morning from Hawaii (6 hours earlier).

Try and get a list with FAX numbers as well as phone numbers, if you can. It makes for a great sales presentation to have the customer holding a picture of your book surrounded by sales buzzwords and great review news when you call.

But, suppose what you wrote is so unique that no lists for stores dealing in that topic exist. Contact the magazine which sells directly to the people who might be interested in your book. Say, for example, you wrote about Europe. Locate a magazine dealing with your topic. In *Writers' Market* you will find a magazine entitled, *Europe*. Its circulation is 50,000. Call them and ask them to piggy-back mail for you. Buy their list of subscribers, if you can. Six cents a name is the going rate. Then get the editor to run a review of your book, buy some advertising in the magazine, and call the subscribers to sell a "special" deal.

If you will do your own phone work, (and you should), shop around for a long distance service. Some charge more for daytime calls, less for after-hour. Others cost more to use locally, but less for long distance. Study the ways in which you can cut down on phone costs so you don't start off with a huge phone bill.

Then, **write out** your phone pitch. Use your computer, and hit your customer with your best in the first 15 words. Make sure not to confuse customer benefits with dealer benefits. In our case, we sell the most advanced outdoor information in the world, but we seldom mention that. Even though our books have hot information, the dealer doesn't give a rip. He is motivated by profit, so our pitch tells him he doubles his money, attracts extra customers, and occupies less than a foot of shelf space when he uses our free book rack.

Read your pitch into a tape recorder. If it doesn't sound natural, either practice until you are smooth or re-write it. The customer can't know you are reading.

Keep track of your sales calls on your computer. If you don't know how to Data Base, use a word processor. Print out your files, work on paper, and transcribe your notes every so often so you can print out a fresh, updated work book. For example,  record your calls like this in a main "diary" file:

Joe's wholesale surplus, 1111 Main St, Oakland, CA, 94201. Spoke with  Mary Sue, the buyer. 14 April. Sent EKB lst class. Call 9 Nov. / 415-937-2456.

It takes about two hours to produce ten good "sample-sent-on-request" leads. Use first-class mail.

Fourth-class shows no class and by the time the parcel arrives, the buyer forgot both you **and** your company.

### DON'T SEND ONLY THE STEAK; SEND THE SIZZLE

Sending only your book won't work. Most buyers for stores often spend less than three minutes "reading" your book, so a good cover letter gets better results by drawing their attention to your best sales points. Send copies of your reviews, a brochure, and your sales track record. You'll get better results.

In the case of our Green Beret series, the local military store says they can't keep them in stock. That's a great endorsement. We quote that often, especially when we are trying to establish a new account. Also, now that we've been around so long, we offer to take a return on books not sold.

Standard sales procedure for any salesman includes this rule: Never ask any question to which the buyer can answer, "no." On the second call, don't ask outright if the buyer read your book, because 90% don't.

Do whatever you have to do to make the first sale. On one deal, we paid the freight to New York. We took a killer introductory price from another wholesaler. (But my books are out there.)

No matter what your sales pitch is, timing the close is important. You have to ask the customer to spend money. In our case, we sell introductory packages to dealers at a discount. Also, I offer dealers a sales leader; my Hammock book wholesales for $2.98. Once they place a small order, the more expensive books are easier to sell.

Over half of the retail store owners who take our samples become dealers. Once the books are in a store and selling well, all we have to do is maintain the dealerships. Generally, we supply window displays, book display racks, and free review copy for local media. We call our dealers bi-monthly.

Tele-marketing not only gives you direct access to big dollar sales with your books; it also helps you write product. We ask questions on the phone and get back lots of tips, ranging from product information to news on where we can sell a lot more. Using the phone is a great way to go. Calling my dealers back now is like calling old friends. When all is said and done, the telephone is the best sales tool a publisher can use.

Sales start with a good subject, and then develop when you begin calling on the markets. With a decent product, some sincere promotional writing, and your personal attention on the phone, you can make your book take off on the sales charts.

Writing the product is so much more enjoyable when you know there is an eager world waiting to buy. As soon as you print, jump on the phone and set up your dealers. A good income will be yours for years to come.

*Helvetica  12 pt*

## GLOSSARY

**Baud.** Speed at which computer language travels over phone.

**Clamshell.** v.t. Scoop into a manuscript and lift portions out which will become separate chapters of text on their own.

**double entendre.** Double meaning of one word or phrase which surprises reader and makes her laugh.

**DBase.** Data base---software for a computer. You store information, names, addresses, phone numbers, etc., in a manner much the same as index cards. After storing, you can sort and call them by zip, age, male/female, etc.

**Files.** Named after a file in a file cabinet. Files are collected groups of related information stored on a computer disc.

**Filler.** Writing or illustrations to expand your book to match printer signature specs. Also used to make page attractive.

**Font.** A style of letter assigned to a whole alphabet. Includes styling for lower case, CAPS, *italics*, **bold**, shadow and outline letters, plus combinations of the above. MacIntosh computers generate all styles of each font design.

**Font size.** Measured in points, it means how big a letter is. Note, different sizes for different fonts are not the same size.

**Green Beret.** Army soldiers in Special Forces named after a kind of hat they wear who are trained to use silk to float down into strange, beautiful, exotic lands, encounter wonderful people from a different culture, and kill them.

**@#$%^&** adjective used to describe lawn mowers which don't work and government officials who won't.

**Gringos** Formerly, a derogatory name for North Americans with lots of money, but little heart. Latin attitude has improved, but the word hasn't yet become term of endearment.

**Karate.** Art of open hand. Much like writing---art of open mind. Achieve depends on how hard you train and go for it.

**M.O.** Modus Operandi. Normally attributed to criminals who operate by repeating same method as they plunder our citizenry. Here, it simply means, how I do it.

**New York minute**. Sixty seconds of time occurring three hours before California clocks know it happened, and six hours ahead of Hawaii, where we don't care if it happened. But we heard it happens awfully quick...

**Pizazz**. Allurement created by make-up, baubles and polish. In writing, clever use of language, topic order, humor, etc.

**Polish**. What wood-workers do to make it shine, and what word-workers do for the same effect. This book got 13 coats, two of which were automatic, three of which were supervised, and the rest of which were hand, elbow-grease rub-outs.

**Popcorn**. v.t. Means to blow up text and expand it.

**Saddle**. Leather seat on a horse. Difficult to climb into after having been thrown into dirt and landed hard. For writers, leather thing in front of computer. Frequently much more difficult to mount.

**Scratch outline**. Baby Table of Contents with only descriptive titles for groups of related ideas. Enables you to jockey groups around to achieve maximum sales impact. Sometimes, you rearrange the scratch so your reader gets progressively related information.

**Segue** . To slide smoothly from one topic of writing into another. Used in comedic presentation to keep the listener surprised, and therefore, laughing.

**Self-Publishing**. The highest form of entrepreneurship. You write, edit, and do what we teach in Book II, then sell your books. Result: Either fame by Friday or shame by Shundy.

**Seriff**. The little hook on the end of some letters in a set of fonts. Makes reading difficult, but has eye appeal. Sans = without; sans-seriff refers to fonts without the little hook.

**Shundy**. Seventh day of week pronounced by inebriate after readers shun her. Followed by Maudlundy.

**Waikiki**. Place on island of Oahu where I lived. Long rolling waves. Tennis courts. Hotel rooms: 27,000+ Lovely churches. Soft breezes and music. Aaaah. It's a tough life...

**Writer's block**. Sometimes incurable disease caused by fear of Shundy and the day after, Maudlundy.

**Zinger**. A word or phrase in your book which will astound, electrify and lure readers. You extract your best for your covers (back and front) of your book. Zingers may also be graphics. When you draw a winner, place it where it will be seen by many. Sample graphic zinger: Path on map showing quasi-circular travel and bee-line return to starting point used in *Never Get Lost* by Don Paul. $9.95 before discount.

# HOW TO WRITE A BOOK IN 53 DAYS

# INDEX

DON PAUL

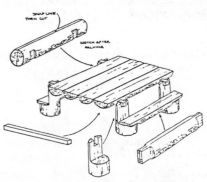

# GREAT LIVIN' IN GRUBBY TIMES

The tricks and techniques found in this book are written by supermen but, anyone can use them and become a master-outdoorsman.

Carriage bolts with big washers fasten the joints. It's easy to make the camper's dream. Cut all the poles from the straight limbs off any tree. It takes down in minutes, and all the poles lay side by side in your pickup. The flat piece in the back is held by chain or rope, and can be used for desk, workbench, table, or counter top for the cook.

While we were at it, we invented the desk that can't be stolen. Or, if somebody does pick it up and carry it off, be very polite to them.

We started with a log. After flattening the bottom, we held a level line at the seat and spray painted on top of newspaper wrapped over a straight edge. After boring into the log with the chainsaw, we merely cut on the bottom of the paint line to make nice seat.

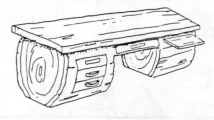

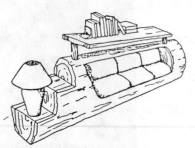

**You can't survive today with old methods and ancient skills. If you're going to make it, you better learn the new ways. This book contains those new ways.**

See how the experts *Choose a Survival Firearm.* Learn how to make *Handmade Weapons,* choose a *Survival Habitat,* and then outfit with *Great Gear for Grubby Times.* Finally, start from scratch and build shelter and furniture with a *Chainsaw,* and then defend it against anything with *Combat Gunnery.* Illustrated, 134 pages for *$12.95*

## By Pathfinder
### New-Method Books For Real Outdoorsmen

# TEAR OUT OR COPY THIS PAGE
## USE YOUR PRODUCT REBATE COUPONS JUST LIKE CASH WHEN YOU ORDER FROM PATH FINDER

Path Finder's product rebate coupons (reverse side) can be used as cash at most of our dealers or by mail order from Path Finder Publications on any of the following:

**NEVER GET LOST. P.A.U.L. system. The Green Beret's Compass Course.** Reviewed by almost every major outdoor magazine, this book contains your land navigation system of the future. You can go anywhere, anytime, **without a map**, and never get lost. We've sold over 25,000 of these and have hundreds of testimonials letters from Alaskan bush pilots to Search and Rescue.    Price before coupon discount: **$9.95**

**EVERYBODY'S KNIFE BIBLE.**   First reviewed by the *AMERICAN SURVIVAL GUIDE MAGAZINE*. They called it "innovative, funny, and sixteen of the most inventive and informative chapters on knives and knife uses ever written." This is **the book** to own if you want to perform like a woods-king in the outdoors with your knife.
Price before coupon discount:  **$12.95**

**AMMO FOREVER.** Total self sufficiency for every gun you own. By Huber. June 92. Simplifies reloading for all gun types. When the government shuts off supply, this book will keep your guns loaded.
Price before coupon discount: **$12.95**

**EVERYBODY'S OUTDOOR SURVIVAL GUIDE. The Green Beret's Guide to Outdoor Survival.** Over 15,000 in print with great reviews. This book teaches you survival arts as if you were on a Green Beret team. Best shooting instruction around for all weapons.  It has Woodcroft's hand-to-hand combat methods, water purification. Also, how to double your survive-ability by using animals, plus more.
Price before coupon discount: **$12.95**

**GREAT LIVIN' IN GRUBBY TIMES. The Green Beret's Guide #2.** No other book ever taught weapons selection for survival like this one. It has combat shooting and the legendary Brian Adam's ESCAPE AND EVASION  plus too much more to mention. We've sold over 10,000.
Price before coupon discount: **$12.95**

**SPEED SPANISH FOR GRINGOS, The World's fastest get-you-fluent Spanish Book.** Contains Welfare Mentality Method for getting vocabulary: *"Don't work for it; steal it."*  Available Ap92. **$12.95**

**Note:** All Path Finder books are guaranteed for life. Destroy one or buy a new upgrade, and pay only half for the latest and greatest.

# These a‌_____ues.

They work just th‌_____ to purchase
Path Finder Books.

---

FROM: _____

_____      ____/____/____
                                    date
_____

Pay to the order of: <u>Path Finder Publications  //  $2.50</u>

<u>Two dollars and fifty cents</u>

For: <u>BOOKS</u>                    _____

---

FROM: _____

_____      ____/____/____
                                    date
_____

Pay to the order of: <u>Path Finder Publications  //  $2.50</u>

<u>Two dollars and fifty cents</u>

For: _____

---

NOTIC‌_____ ‌oks are
guara‌_____ with our
latest ‌

*DEAL‌_____ one value
cash or‌

Mail‌                                    ‌5

MGib